# THE SECRET TUNNELS
## *of*
# SOUTH HEIGHTON

## A Tribute to HMS FORWARD
## Newhaven Royal Naval Headquarters

### GEOFFREY ELLIS

S. B. Publications

*This book is dedicated to the crew of HMS FORWARD who wore headphones, not helmets; who brandished Morse keys not machine guns; who used teleprinters, not torpedos; despatching bulletins, not bullets; and who contemplated the courses of clandestine convoys in secret silence.*

**They too contributed to the Defence of the Realm and the winning of the War**

First published in 1996 by S.B. Publications
c/o 19 Grove Road, Seaford, East Sussex BN25 1TP.
*Reprinted 1996*

ISBN 1 85770 101 1

Typeset, printed and bound by MFP Design & Print
Longford Trading Estate, Thomas Street, Stretford, Manchester M32 0JT

# CONTENTS

Front Cover: *Eastern Descent into HMS FORWARD tunnels.* (Tom Bonnor, 1993)

Inset: *Scene in the Plotting room, 1944.* (Geoffrey Ellis; ©1994)

Back Cover: *"Sappers" finishing off one of the long stairways leading to an exit.* (© IWM; Photo H 14508, 2 October 1941)

# PREFACE

There have been many accounts of the tremendous efforts made by the Armed Forces to bring about the successful outcome of the Second World War, but none has credited the contributions made by hundreds of servicemen and women who maintained a constant vigil deep beneath Heighton Hill, Newhaven, in an intensely secret intelligence centre known as HMS FORWARD and NOIC NEWHAVEN. The author, South Heighton born and bred, wishes to redress this long standing injustice by publicly revealing the facts.

Intelligence, or knowledge, is vital in wartime, and cannot be acquired without observation and communication. It is essential to know exactly where the enemy is and what he is proposing to do, and how he is seeking to achieve his aims. It is no less essential to know exactly where your own resources are deployed in the theatre of war at any instant, and to be able to communicate with them if the need arises.

Any establishment which accumulates and disseminates such information is a vital control centre and if discovered by the enemy, features high on his hit list. Such locations are therefore made as inconspicuous, impregnable, and as secret as possible. This then is the scenario in which HMS FORWARD operated. For fifty years I have hoped that somebody who served there would record for posterity the purpose, activities and history of HMS FORWARD, but nobody ever has; and since I doubt now that they ever will, I therefore feel I must.

I dedicate this work to all those who served here during the war; to those who wore headphones, not helmets, and who brandished Morse keys, not machine guns; to those who coded and decoded the messages; to those who plotted the nautical movements; to those who operated teleprinters or telephone switchboards; and to the runners and Officers who supported their efforts. May the fruits of my research help to alleviate the injustice of silence served on this establishment by the destruction of official records following its abandonment in 1945.

Today nature has joined forces with the developers to eradicate the final external vestiges of a vital secret wartime communications centre. Substantial undergrowth and overgrowth now covers the only remaining external evidence of its existence, all other signs having succumbed to the developer's pneumatic drill. No longer ventilated, the air inside is saturated, and condensation drips from every surface. The tunnel is deemed to remain silent for all time; unseen even by those who live closest to it.

This Naval Headquarters ought to be nominated an Ancient Monument for our heritage, even more deservedly than many other historic fortifications built to Defend the Realm but never used in anger. It is not too late to preserve what does remain, and there are cogent reasons for doing so.

# ABOUT THE AUTHOR

I was born in 4 Russell Terrace (now 174 Avis Road), and lived there until 1954. When I was five years of age in 1939, I went to South Heighton village school, in Miss Hooper's class. Miss Hooper taught the younger pupils in the more northerly classroom. The days were spent learning the alphabet, learning how to count, learning the 'times tables', painting with water colours, singing, and listening to moralist tales about Brer Rabbit.

I was taken to school and collected by my mother, walking along the Beddingham road. An alternative route led along the top of the bank parallel to the road which I used later when I went to school on my own or with friends. Either route led directly past the site destined for excavating the labyrinth beneath Heighton hill, and when the work began in 1941, I saw the activities being conducted beneath copious canopies of camouflage.

Children knew there was a war on. Rationing limited our food, and more importantly, sweets for me and my sister. Besides the air raids, there was barbed wire and rows of small concrete pyramids called 'dragons teeth' everywhere. A local policeman came to the school on occasions to show pictures of things we were told we must never touch, such as grenades, butterfly bombs and anti-personnel devices, and told us to report any such items to an adult without delay.

I remember those early war years for their long hot summers. The introduction of Double British Summer Time meant changing the clocks forward an hour twice in the spring, and retarding them an hour twice in the autumn. This effectively reduced the hours of darkness and saved electrical power for the war effort. In practice it meant that it stayed daylight until eleven o'clock at night, and it was difficult to persuade children it was bedtime when the sun was still high in the sky. It was so in the summer of 1941 when the tunnel was being built, because I remember vividly certain events which occurred of an evening.

It must be remembered that the enemy had occupied Northern France since June, 1940, and planned to invade England as the next step in his conquests (Operation Sealion). Enemy aerial reconnaissance was a constant threat and precautions were necessary to avoid drawing attention to the constructional works being carried out on this undeveloped hillside. No spillage of chalk on the metalled road surface could be tolerated, nor any signs of heavy vehicles having crossed virgin downland pasture.

Whilst the tunnel was being excavated, work began beneath an expanse of camouflage on the hillside behind Portland Terrace where four large circular holes were dug into the chalk. Soldiers were busily working, mixing and laying concrete, putting up corrugated-iron shuttering and pouring copious quantities of concrete into the shuttering with iron reinforcing rods embedded. What attracted me (and others) most of all, was the narrow-gauge miner's tramway they used to carry the vast quantities of cement, sand, aggregate, and reinforcing rods from the top of the hill down to these sites, to avoid disfiguring the hillside.

It was great fun of an evening to ride those rugged miners trams down the gentle slope of the hillside. The track down the path to the first pillbox ended with a turntable from which the track led across the hillside at right angles to the path. We therefore had to jump off the tram before reaching this point as the momentum of the freewheeling wagon carried it across the turntable to become momentarily airborne where the track finished. The soldiers who had to rerail their wagons in the morning probably had an uncomplimentary name for us.

When the pillboxes were completed the track was lifted and the camouflage was removed. After a while the intense constructional activity at the tunnel mouth subsided leaving only an armed sentry on duty at the gate. I recall talking to the sentries on my journeys to and from school; I suppose they were pleased to break the monotony of watching the grass grow.

Early in 1946 a friend rather excitedly told me the tunnel gate was open. He had seen some other lads go in — had I got a torch? We went in and looked around. It was an intensely exciting adventure into the unknown. There was lots of masonry debris on the floor, and damp plywood hung from the breeze-block partitioning. Lengths of air-conditioning trunking littered the floor and electrical conduits dangled crazily from the roof. Everywhere was a scene of desecration.

Wandering around we came upon some concrete steps. One flight led up to a securely locked and bolted grilled iron gate; another flight led up to a vertical shaft containing a long wooden ladder which we climbed and found ourselves looking out of the chicken shed. Elsewhere in the tunnel we climbed flights of wooden stairs and discovered that these led to the four hillside pillboxes.

The most interesting part of the labyrinth was the middle part where the tunnels were much larger, with signs of heavy machinery having been mounted on concrete plinths. There were some discarded tiny accumulators laying around (In the 1940s, few houses in South Heighton had mains electricity; in consequence all domestic radios were battery operated and used accumulators which had to be recharged every week. I was very familiar with these devices). My most treasured discovery was a ganged variable capacitor which I later used to construct my first crystal set.

All the galleries looked alike — save for two instances. In one gallery were two pits about two-feet deep in the floor, one with a step. These pits were most intriguing and I then postulated that this contained a generator installation. The other gallery of note contained a couple of small offices. I recall a wooden plaque on one office door signwritten "Col. Cheeseman".

We made further visits to satisfy our quests for adventure and curiosity. The labyrinth was complex, and it was essential to remember where you were. The mental picture created then remained with me for nearly fifty years. In 1992 I drew a convincingly accurate sketch of the system which formed the basis of the case for making a detailed archaeological type survey whilst it was still possible to enter the tunnels.

I left Lewes County Grammar School in 1951 and took a career with GPO Telephones. This involved a two year apprenticeship studying for City and Guilds Technical Examinations in specialist subjects. I completed my apprenticeship with a very comprehensive indoctrination into the fundamental principles and practice of telecommunications.

In 1953 I joined Her Majesty's Royal Air Force for my National Service. My civilian professional qualifications decreed that I train as a "Line Telegraph Fitter" to recondition and maintain the RAF's telegraph equipment. The RAF proposed to support its own teleprinter communications equipment, formerly maintained by the GPO, and needed technicians immediately.

I was posted to RAF Compton Bassett in Wiltshire on a six-week Basic Electricity course studying telecommunications principles and practice once more, followed by a thirty-eight-week comprehensive training course on teleprinters, auto-transmitters, perforators, reperforators, printing reperforators, line signalling and multichannel voice signalling (MCVF) equipment. The course included training on (the then) secret Typex cryptographic machines. At the end of the course we could strip down and rebuild any of these machines, and had to prove it in a practical examination. It was a very intensive course, but as we completed our training, the RAF abrogated its proposals, and instantly created six redundant tradesmen.

The RAF decided to retrain us as Instructors and promptly sent us to RAF Spitalgate on a lecturing course. The rest of my National Service was spent at RAF Compton Bassett and then RAF Locking lecturing telecommunications theory and first-line teleprinter equipment maintenance to new recruits and Officers.

I was interested in radio when at school but whilst I was at RAF Compton Bassett I did some serious study and construction work. I had access to a radio laboratory where I learned the Morse Code using a Wheatstone transmitter. Lecturing presented me with lots of free time between lectures which I used to advantage and I passed my GPO Morse examination at Burnham Radio Station.

I acquired my Radio Amateur Licence in 1956 and have actively enjoyed this hobby ever since. When Mr Reg Snelling, who lived in 12 West View Terrace, learned of my newly acquired licence, he presented me with a very sturdy aerial mast which he had obtained from the Admiralty — it had been in use at HMS FORWARD during the war! That mast is still standing in 1996, the only surviving remnant which is still in active service!

Throughout my subsequent professional career with GPO Telephones, PO Telephones, and British Telecommunications (the same firm, just different headed note paper!) I have worked on a great variety of equipment including telephones, teleprinters, telephone exchanges, line transmission equipment, telegraph terminals, and power plant equipment (batteries, rectifiers, and stand-by engines). During these years I attended twelve technical courses relating to the above equipment practices.

In 1964 I learned of proposals to further develop Heighton Hill, and by way of making a personal memento of what remained of the tunnel, I took some black and white pictures of the hillside pillboxes and the tunnel entrance as they were then, looking much the same as they did twenty years earlier. A colleague developed the film and produced a set of contact proof prints which I kept for some twenty eight years. Those photographs are the only known pictures of the tunnel surface structures before demolition by the developers creating Glynde Close and Heighton Crescent.

In March, 1991, the dreaded recession resulted in my being made redundant. I found myself in a veritable ocean of unemployed manpower. My experience in such a specialised sphere counted for nothing, and I became a statistic . . .

A chance remark about the tunnel to Peter Bailey (Curator of Newhaven Museum) during a slide show on 13 October, 1992, and mention of my 1964 pictures resulted in an approach to Peter Vandenbegin (Local Manager, Guinness Trust Estates).

The outcome has been the opportunity for me to live in a time-warp where I have been able to direct my knowledge and experience of telecommunications, together with the reminiscences of those who served there during the war, to recreate an authentic record of the purpose and practices of HMS FORWARD, never before fully revealed.

Here then, are the facts that were nearly lost for all time.

A video cassette by the same title compliments this book with a tour of the tunnels in great detail, and includes interviews with some of the veterans who served here during the War. The video is available from the author c/o S.B. Publications

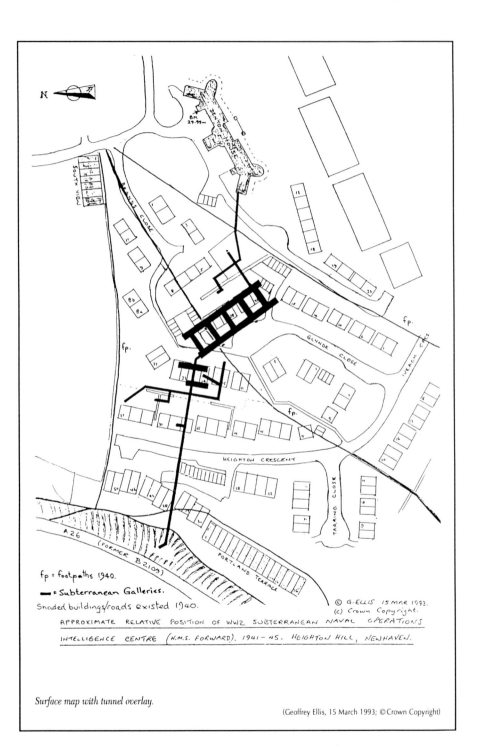

N

fp = footpaths 1940.

━ = Subterranean Galleries.

Shaded buildings/roads existed 1940.

© G. ELLIS 15 MAR 1993.
(c) Crown Copyright.

APPROXIMATE RELATIVE POSITION OF WW2 SUBTERRANEAN NAVAL OPERATIONS INTELLIGENCE CENTRE (H.M.S. FORWARD). 1941-45. HEIGHTON HILL, NEWHAVEN.

*Surface map with tunnel overlay.*

(Geoffrey Ellis, 15 March 1993; © Crown Copyright)

8

# ON-SITE SURVEYS AND RESEARCH

Following a slide show of old Sussex given by Peter Bailey, Hon. Curator of Newhaven Local & Maritime Museum to a Toc-H meeting at Searchlight Workshops on 13 October, 1992, I asked him what he knew about the former wartime tunnel beneath Heighton Hill. I showed him my photographs of surface artifacts taken in 1964.

Peter made enquiries and discovered persons living locally who had served there during the war; and the Officer charged with its design resided in Seaford. It was learned that one entrance to the subterranean communications centre emerged within Denton House (Originally known as The Guinness Trust Holiday Home).

Guinness Trust Estate Manager Mr Peter Vandenbegin was approached with a view to investigating the access from (the then vacant) Denton House. He was unaware of the association of Denton House with the tunnel and he joined the growing number of enthusiasts anxious to know more. It was proposed to research and record as much information as possible for the sake of posterity to correct an injustice which has existed for nearly fifty years. Peter Vandenbegin wrote to the Trustees explaining the situation, requesting their approval for a limited exploration.

On 10 December, 1992, a small group gathered at Denton House for a preliminary assessment of the facts. The plan was to identify the entrance to the tunnel. One particular room had a painted concrete slab replacing some missing parquet flooring, and sounded hollow beneath. During examination the thickness of this slab was found to be rather inadequate and potentially dangerous.

*Newhaven Museum Curator Peter Bailey and Constable Mel Allen stand on reinstated flooring which disguised the main tunnel entrance for forty-seven years.*

(Geoffrey Ellis, 10 December 1992)

9

*The hole in the floor made with a one-pound hammer(!) revealing the void with fourteen steps to the solid brick wall (erected 21 November 1945) sealing the tunnel.*

(Geoffrey Ellis, 10 December 1992)

It took only a few taps with a one-pound hammer to penetrate the floor and disclose a 7ft (2m) void below. Within seconds the hole was enlarged sufficiently to reveal a dozen steps down to a solid brick wall. It was like Tutenkhamun revisited.

Satisfied that the entrance had been found, further investigation was postponed pending authority from the Guinness Trust Estates. A potential major accident hazard was averted by the survey; the frailty of the concrete floor was an accident waiting to happen. It was now apparent that when the tunnel was sealed in 1945, the floor was reinstated by fixing horizontal battens to the walls of the stairway, and laying planking between them to support a layer of concrete which was to form the floor. At the time, the woodwork was more substantial than the concrete it carried, but over the years dry rot had completely decayed the timber leaving the concrete unsupported. It was under an inch thick in one area!

On 4 January, 1993, I wrote to the Imperial War Museum to enquire what they knew about this underground establishment. A few days later Peter Simkins, of the IWM Research & Information Office rang me to question my information. He lived in Brighton and had made a study of Sussex WW2 establishments. He was sure I meant Newhaven Fort, and was amazed when I mentioned the commemorative plaque in Denton House.

In a letter dated 14 January he replied "Further to your letter of 4 January and our telephone conversation two days later, I have now had an opportunity to check our records for references to the former underground communications post and headquarters at Newhaven. Although I have looked for material under the various names of these headquarters, including HMS FORWARD, Denton House and even the Guinness Trust Holiday Home, very little has so far come to light in our collections . . . Whilst there is no specific mention of Newhaven on the index cards compiled by our Department of Documents on Naval shore establishments and Headquarters, the Keeper of that department reminded me that we do have the papers of Vice-Admiral J. Hughes-Hallett, who commanded the Naval forces in the Dieppe raid. Since you believe that the Newhaven establishments were involved in the Dieppe Raid, it may be worth your while to come and have a look at this collection to see if it contains any evidence on the headquarters which are the subject of your research". He concluded his letter by suggesting that I seek the advice of the Naval Historical Branch of the Ministry of Defence.

This I did, and in a letter dated 25 January, D. Ashby of the MOD wrote "Thank you for your letter of 19 January, 1993, regarding a shore establishment at Newhaven. I regret that we are unable to undertake research on behalf of the public and I am therefore unable to answer your question . . . The Ministry of Defence does not, in fact, hold on to records that are over thirty years old. All Admiralty documents dealing with events that occurred more than thirty years ago and which have been thought worthy of preservation are held in the custody of the Public Record Office, Kew . . . I am sorry that I have not been able to be more helpful."

*View of the floor hole enlarged for access, and of the hole through wall.*

(Geoffrey Ellis, 27 January 1993)

Mr Ian Everest, Manager of Newhaven Fort subsequently revealed that the IWM does have some unique photographs of "577 Army Field Coy REs at Denton, Nr Seaford" showing "An underground operation control centre now under construction somewhere in the SE Command". These photographs (IWM refs H.14501 to H.14508) are attributed to Lieut. Tanner, 2 October, 1941, and are identifiable.

Meanwhile qualified approval of our request to gain entry into the tunnel through Denton House had been granted by the Guinness Trust Estates, and attentions were directed towards the far more interesting prospects of surveying the tunnel interior for such period as we had freedom of access. On Monday, 18 January, 1993, Peter Bailey, Cyril Leister and I entered the tunnel following three days considerable efforts by Cyril and others to make a hole in the brick wall which sealed this entrance to the tunnel. It was 9ins (230mm) thick, built with engineering bricks, and bore the date 21 November, 1945 (a Wednesday), cast in wet cement by the thoughtful bricklayer.

## Beyond the wall

It was clear from the grafitti beyond the wall that the tunnel had been visited many times over the decades by others entering by the western entrance. Looting, adventure, and curiosity seem to have been the primary objectives. Unsuccessful efforts had been made to breach the wall in the opposite direction, and vain attempts had been made to retrieve some bronze flanges attached to some pneumatic message tubing.

The structure of the tunnel, once lined, is now exposed. Strong pairs of curved steel joists, fishplated at the top, and linked to the next with iron bars, support heavily galvanised corrugated iron sheeting which is moulded to the contours of the joists. Formerly this ironwork was hidden by a lining of white-washed bitumen roofing felt at this entrance. The tattered remains of this now festoon the empty cable-trays, pneumatic tubes and hand rails like so much dirty washing. The concrete floor and stairs shine with the wetness from which they are no longer protected.

*Plan of tunnel. East end.*  (Geoffrey Ellis, 20 December 1995)

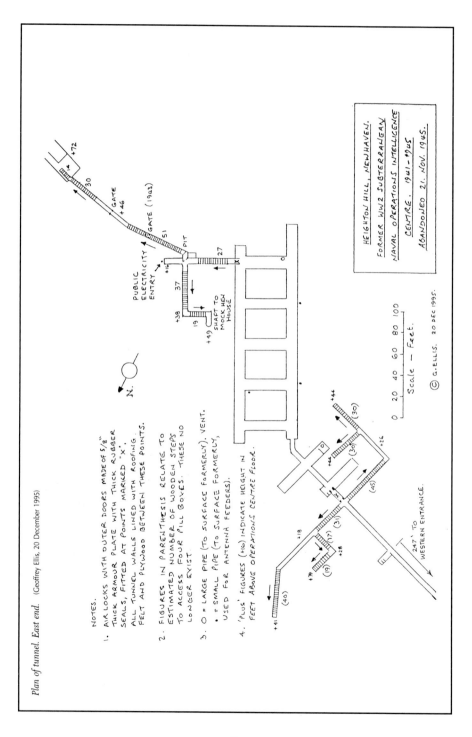

NOTES.

1. AIR LOCKS WITH OUTER DOORS MADE OF 5/8"
THICK ARMOUR PLATE WITH THICK RUBBER
SEALS, FITTED AT POINTS MARKED "X".
ALL TUNNEL WALLS LINED WITH ROOFING.
FELT AND PLYWOOD BETWEEN THESE POINTS.

2. FIGURES IN PARENTHESIS RELATE TO
ESTIMATED NUMBER OF WOODEN STEPS
TO ACCESS FOUR PILL BOXES. THESE NO
LONGER EXIST.

3. O = LARGE PIPE (TO SURFACE FORMERLY). VENT.
• = SMALL PIPE (TO SURFACE FORMERLY,
USED FOR ANTENNA FEEDERS).

4. 'PLUS' FIGURES (+16) INDICATE HEIGHT IN
FEET ABOVE OPERATIONS CENTRE FLOOR.

N.

HEIGHTON HILL, NEWHAVEN.
FORMER WW2 SUBTERRANEAN
NAVAL OPERATIONS INTELLIGENCE
CENTRE. 1941-1945
ABANDONED 21. NOV. 1945.

Scale — Feet.
0   20   40   60   80   100

© G. ELLIS.   20 DEC 1995.

+72
30
GATE
+46
51
GATE (1943)
PUBLIC
ELECTRICITY
ENTRY
PIT
+16
37
27
+38
19
+49
SHAFT TO
MOCK HEN
HOUSE

+44
(30)
+44
(30)
+26
(45)
X
(31)
+18
+39
(19)
(17)
+28
(40)
+41
247' TO
WESTERN ENTRANCE.

Descending the stairs and passing through two stout grilled iron gates, one on a landing and another halfway down the next flight of stairs, one cannot fail to be impressed by the approach into the depths below. These are not rough concrete steps underfoot, but well-fashioned smooth stairs with a rounded nose. There is a sense of quality about both the workmanship and materials in the interior which does not escape notice today. Considering the haste with which this centre would have been needed, those who laboured to excavate and construct the interior would have been under some pressure to complete. Their work stands testimony to their craftsmanship, and will probably do so for all time. The brickwork linings of the grenade trap, machine gun posts, and the air-lock pillars are but a few examples to be appreciated.

At the foot of a flight of fifty-one stairs, across the entire width of the passage, is a grenade trap about 6ft (2m) deep which once had a strong removable wooden cover. Immediately beyond this is the recessed gun port of the machine gun post with its 4ft thick wall. Here the passage turns to the right to meet a landing with a flight of stairs ascending ahead; another flight of stairs descends to the left, and to the right is a small chamber. The stairs ahead lead up to a 20ft vertical shaft to the mock chicken house observation post which also contained an escape hatch for use in case of damage to the east and west exits of the tunnel.

The flight of twenty-seven stairs descending from the landing, with the machine gun post access on the left, leads down to the strongly protected operations area. Here at the foot of the stairs, some 60ft (18m) below the surface and 72ft (22m) below the entrance level, is an armour plate steel door 5ft 8ins x 2ft 8ins x 0.625ins (1.727 x 0.812 x 0.016m) thick weighing more than 3cwt (156kg), set in engineering brick pillars 2ft (0.61m) square. The door, supported by two massive hinges, closed against its metal frame on a one inch thick cylindrical neoprene rubber seal which still remains spongy and pliable fifty years later.

Originally this door contained a 3ins (75mm) diameter window made from two pieces of Georgian wired glass. This tiny window must have proved inadequate because it was later enlarged by drilling a large number of adjacent holes around the circumference of a 7.5ins (200mm) diameter

*The scene beyond the wall. Decaying timber no longer supports the white-faced bituminous felt which droops over hand-rails. The severed pneumatic tube is wedged behind the hand-rail.*

(Geoffrey Ellis, 25 January 1993)

*The second security gate half way down a flight of 51 steps installed in 1943. The gate was 'split' to avoid the steps and sloping roof. Braby cable-tray on wall carried telephone cables. The stair 'risers' were whitewashed regularly. The notice "NOT FIT FOR DRINKING" was discovered in the tunnel.*

(Geoffrey Ellis, 25 January 1993)

*Grenade pit & machine gun post. A machine gun at the bottom of the four feet long square gun port would have dealt whithering fire up the fifty-one-step stairway.*

(Tom Bonnor, 1993)

circle and then joining the holes with a saw blade. The 'core' of this hole, complete with tiny window, was discovered in the fan room where it had been left by the luckless individual who had to execute this task. When it was discovered, and 'offered up' to the steel door, it fitted like Cinderella's glass slipper! Whatever was substituted in the larger hole was later deemed desirable, for that too has since disappeared!

This was the outer door of an air-lock designed to protect against bomb blast and maintain the tunnel interior air pressure; there was another less substantial door to the air-lock just 6ft (2m) inside. Only small cable ducts, electrical conduits and valved pressure relief ports about 4ins (100mm) square perforated the door pillars. Both doors were normally kept closed despite a considerable amount of trafficking through them.

The operations centre consists of two parallel galleries approximately 9ft wide, 8ft high and 190ft long (2·7 x 2·4 x 58m) about 50ft (15·2m) apart, aligned roughly north/south. Five galleries of similar bore connect them at regular intervals of 39ft (11·9m), running roughly east/west. These galleries formed the nerve centre of the intelligence unit.

*East air-lock. Showing dismembered armour plate door, pneumatic message tube, braby cable tray, pressure relief vent, and a recessed light fitting frame.*

(Geoffrey Ellis, 25 January 1993)

Located here were the radio receivers, teleprinters, telephone switchboards, plotting table, cipher office, and all manner of associated equipment. There was also sleeping accommodation for Officers and Ratings. Nearby was a galley, an emergency generator, and an air-conditioning plant. One gallery had two pits about 2ft deep; one contained hundreds of gallons of water which initially defied reasonable explanation.

Breeze-block partitions subdivided the larger galleries into smaller areas. Some partitions remain intact, some are damaged, and others are toppled completely. Best preserved is the suite of cabins for "personnel on day and night watches" at the north end of the western large gallery. Some veterans remembered other areas also being used for sleeping accommodation.

At the north end of the western large gallery a smaller 5ft (1·5m) wide gallery turns left through 45°, and in a few yards passes larger bore galleries on either side. To the left is the emergency generator room, and to the right is the ventilation equipment room both now devoid of machinery but containing evidence of the equipment once installed here and the purpose it served.

The small gallery continues on a few yards, now flanked by air ducts which further reduce the width of the passage. The air ducts temporarily dive below footway level as the gallery passes two more large galleries. This time on the left is the galley or refreshment area, whilst opposite are two toilet cubicles, one of which contained the rusted remains of an Elsan chemical toilet.

Paint lines on the floor of the galley (mess) indicate the former existence of a central partition, probably of timber construction, possibly to separate the Chiefs from the Indians, or even the Army from the Navy? A 6ins (150mm) square duct in the floor conveyed heated air from the fan room. Two

*East main gallery. Wooden Cipher Offices stood right foreground. Passageway on left. Switchboards were just beyond.*

(Tom Bonnor, 1993)

*Teleprinter room. Looking west. Detritus now covers the floor of this room once linked to Dover, Portsmouth, London, and after August '44, ANCXF Paris.*

(Geoffrey Ellis, 15 June 1994)

small pits in the floor reveal that a sink stood here; close by there are remains of a lead water pipe. Remnants of a Mustard Gas Indicator hang on the wall above the door with a pipe into the air-lock behind it.

The existence of grafitti has been mentioned before. Most of it is post-war and fairly innocuous, consisting of names and dates of those who sought to record their visit; some is notable on account of the formation of the letter "A". The author has used a 'square' "A" rather like an "H" with the top crossed. In different places on the walls of the galley, written in this script, appear the texts "SAPPER MATTHEWS" and "CAPE WRATH No 5". These texts can feasibly be ascribed to a Royal Engineer involved in the excavation or construction who wished to be remembered.

Continuing on, the small gallery passes through the west end air-lock, again flanked by the air ducts. Here, electrical conduits hang from the roof where attempts to salvage them have been unsuccessful. The air-lock inner door and its frame were removed to facilitate the evacuation of large and heavy equipment from the tunnel leaving a 4ins (100mm) gap in the flagstone flooring where the threshold stood. This now reveals the underfloor channelling excavated to convey the ducted air past the entrances to the galley and toilets.

The outer door of the west air-lock was another armour plate door mounted on substantial brick pillars. Both the door and frame are now gone; the restricted clearances of this doorway necessitated its removal together with some brickwork to recover the engine and generator.

Embedded in the lintel of the outer air-lock door are the remains of three rubber insulated 14-pair communications type cables. No evidence of their origins or destinations can be traced today. One proceeded along the gallery towards the western entrance, its ultimate destination and purpose unknown. These cables may have provided communication with the pillboxes and western entrance.

No longer within the secure area, immediately beyond the air-lock the small gallery passes two small inclined galleries going left and right, which led to the four hillside pillboxes defending the establishment. Now only slippery bare chalk slopes, they once contained skeleton wooden stairs to

*Western air-lock. The armour plate door and some brickwork was removed to recover the engine and generator. Air trunking on left and right, toilet vent top left. Access to hillside pillboxes leads off left and right.*

(Geoffrey Ellis, 25 January 1993)

*Plan of tunnel. West end.* (Geoffrey Ellis, 30 December 1995)

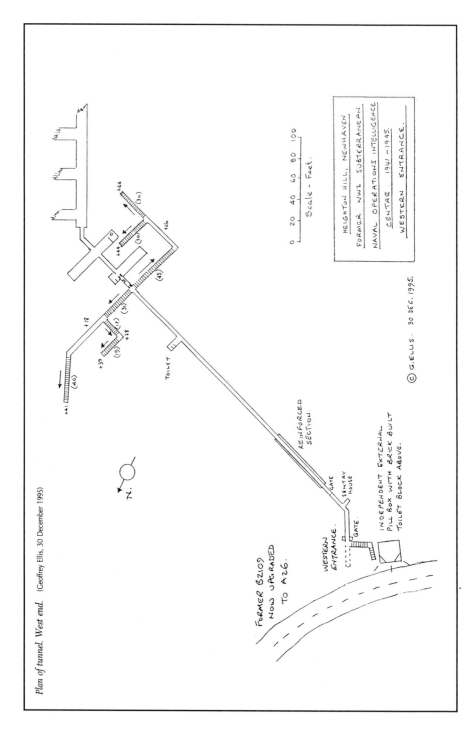

HEIGHTON HILL, NEWHAVEN
FORMER WW2 SUBTERRANEAN
NAVAL OPERATIONS INTELLIGENCE
CENTRE 1941-1945.
WESTERN ENTRANCE.

Scale - Feet.
0   20   40   60   80   100

© G. ELLIS. 30 DEC. 1995.

REINFORCED SECTION.

TOILET

+41 (40)
+39
+18
(19) (17) (30)
+28
+44 (30)
+26
+40 (30)
(45)

N.

FORMER B2109 NOW UPGRADED TO A26.

WESTERN ENTRANCE.
GATE
SENTRY HOUSE
GATE
INDEPENDENT EXTERNAL PILL BOX WITH BRICK BUILT TOILET BLOCK ABOVE.

climb 50ft (15·2m) to the surface. The final 9ft (2·7m) into the pillboxes was ascended by ladders fabricated from unprepared timber.

The pillboxes were demolished when the land was developed. Large and heavy chunks of reinforced concrete which once formed the pillboxes were dropped down the access holes to rest against the decaying ladders. One day the wood will no longer support the weight, and hundredweights of rubble will cascade down the steep chalk slopes to the galleries below.

The small gallery continues on its way towards the western exit, and in 20yds (18m) passes a second two cubicle toilet with a hand washing trough adjacent. The sump associated with this trough still retains the strong scent of disinfectant employed fifty years ago! The gallery carries on in a straight line for a further 68yds (65m), to a point where there is another grilled iron security gate (installed September, 1943).

Throughout the length of this gallery, evidence suggests that high quality galvanised corrugated iron sheet was in short supply as it only occurs overhead. The lower parts of the walls are flagstones set on edge between the RSJs; above them were sheets of standard quality corrugated iron which have now rusted away completely revealing the virgin chalk sides of the tunnel.

Circa 1972 when the hillside above the west entrance was being developed, a 33yds (30m) section of this gallery was reinforced with breeze-blocks and liquid cement. Pieces of thick walled polyethylene pressure pipes employed to inject the silicone cement into the cavity around the tunnel lining now remain imprisoned by the substance which once flowed freely through them, and the solidified dark grey compound can be seen where it attempted to exude from joints in the galvanised corrugated iron sheeting.

Some 7yds (6m) from the 1943 security gate the gallery turns right through 45° where an internal machine gun post formerly protected the west end exit. After another 7yds (6m) the west exit gate is reached, close to the A26 Newhaven — Beddingham road. Two external fights of steps once gave access to the west end toilets and road level.

*Hillside pillbox entry by 9ft vertical ladder now in an advanced state of decay.*
(Tom Bonnor, 1993)

*Western gallery toilet and washing trough. A strong aroma of disinfectant used in these sumps still survives.*
(Tom Bonnor, 1993)

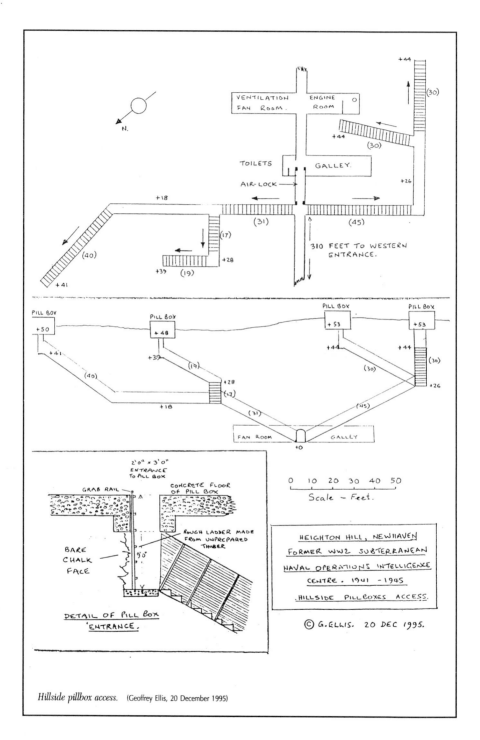

*Hillside pillbox access.* (Geoffrey Ellis, 20 December 1995)

*The author, Geoffrey. Ellis, inspecting decomposed corrugated sheeting in west access gallery. The use of flagstones and standard galvanised iron for the walls indicates a shortage of the high quality galvanised iron used for the roof. These walls were sacrificed as a less important area of the tunnel.*

(Tom Bonnor, 1993)

## Flooring

The operations area floor is paved with 2ft x 3ft (0·6 x 0·9m) flagstones to within about 6ins (150mm) of the walls. The Navy had a penchant for painting white lines along the edges of footways, providing evidence of objects which no longer exist; in one particular instance revealing the location of the cipher office built circa 1943.

## External cables access

Access to the surface for the public electricity supply, antenna leads, stand-by engine exhaust, and foul air vents was by means of lined vertical shafts. Four small 3·5 ins (90mm) diameter pipes were used to carry power and antenna cables, and three larger bore 12ins (300mm) for ventilation. Telephone cables used both the eastern and western exits as mentioned elsewhere.

## Temperature and Humidity

The temperature recorded in the operational area on 28 January, 1993, and was 52·7° Fahrenheit (11·6°C) and remained stable over a number of hours. At this depth, with no other influencing factors the temperature remains constant. As there is no ventilation, the humidity level is consistently high and near dew point. A small drop in external barometric pressure causes a mist to form in the main operational galleries. This was serious enough on occasion to interfere with photography because of back-scatter, and was a constant menace causing condensation on cameras, spectacles and electrical equipment taken into the humid atmosphere below.

## Sounds of today

One might expect that there would be no sound at all to be heard in the tunnel. Certainly there are times when you can actually hear the silence. However, sound does permeate the silence. The unmistakable click of high-heeled shoes on tarmaccadamed road clearly penetrates 25ft of chalk into the gallery approaching Denton House, and carpenters' hammering in Glynde Close has been heard in the deepest depths of the former intelligence centre, albeit considerably muted.

The most common sound is water constantly dripping from any overhead structure onto the detritus laying on the floor. This occurs mainly in the deepest part of the tunnel where the water table tends to be highest, and is especially prevalent following a period of rain; but even during dry spells there is always condensate dripping from the remaining overhead metal trunking. In places little stalactites are growing; and where the flagstones have been removed, the impact of constantly dripping water is eroding small holes in the chalk floor.

The percolating water collects in pools as clean and crystal clear as can be found anywhere. A container, filled to the brim with about 5 gallons (22l) of this sparkling fluid, was later identified to be the enamelled receptacle portion of an Elsan chemical toilet. Fifty years on, it was in a remarkable state of preservation, complete with wooden carrying handle and 'tipping' aid. All those present at the discovery agreed that the water looked good enough to drink; however under the circumstances, volunteers were less forthcoming.

## Artifacts

The Navy did not leave much behind. In 1946 I found a few rolls of multi-ply teleprinter paper, a three-ganged variable capacitor (with which I made my first crystal radio receiver), and some pink Naval Message pads S1320b.

Surprisingly, three unused (and now unusable) rolls of teleprinter paper were found in 1993, one with a pliable green rubber band around it, which had escaped the attentions of many looters and adventurists over the years. Some equipment fuses (GPO Fuses 33A) formerly used on the VF terminal racks were also discovered. These would not be recognised by persons unfamiliar with telecommunications practice.

*Discarded pneumatic pick (puncher) discovered near West airlock. Body of pick is stamped REAVELL & CO LTD. HP2R. 1937 No 486. WD No B205. The bit-retaining collet was broken.*

(Tom Bonnor, 1993)

Without doubt, the most treasured item discovered is the pneumatic pick (known as a puncher). The body of the pick is clearly stamped "REAVELL & Co Ltd., HP2R., 1937, No. 486, W.D. No. B 205". It was cast aside when the bit-retaining clamp broke, and fell down behind some air trunking where it had lain ever since. I wonder whether anybody had to answer for that lost implement.

## The large pits — a revelation

A former wartime telephone engineer, Dennis Tompsett, revealed that the large pits contained GPO telegraph terminal equipment racks which were taller than the tunnel. Owing to the nature of the tunnel the roof could not be raised, so the floor was lowered! The waterproof rendering provided to prevent water draining in from the chalk, today prevents drip water from escaping!

The pits contained vital clues about the equipment, but no way of disposing of 700 gallons (3200l) of water was available. Eventually a self-priming siphon with a half inch bore was left to work for forty-eight hours, slowly discharging the water into the adjacent pit.

The last 1993 visit to the tunnel was Thursday, 11 March, when the final investigations were made. The siphon had worked wonders and drained almost all of the water away. All that remained was a considerable quantity of breeze-block, wood, conduit, anything that earlier visitors had used to make a splash! When all this rubbish and sludge was removed, screw fixing holes in the floor revealed how the racks were sited.

Final photographs of the drained pit were taken to illustrate its shape and depth, before retiring to the surface, removing the temporary floodlighting equipment as we withdrew.

## Further visits of 1994

Information received from WRNS veterans subsequent to the 1993 survey revealed much which had not been appreciated during the initial visits. In particular, the D-Day photograph was discovered,

*The mysterious pit before drainage. January 1993. Geoffrey Ellis provides a conducted tour for Arthur Booker, Maurice Freeman, Don Lewry, Newhaven Mayor Jo Lewry, and Lt Chadwick (veteran HMS FORWARD plotter)*

(Tom Bonnor, 1993)

*The mysterious pit, drained, March 1993, which accommodated telephone equipment racks. Note step at far corner and second pit in background.*

(Tom Bonnor, 1993)

and the true locations of the W/T office and Plotting rooms. There was a need to rephotograph these locations with a different emphasis, and so an appeal was made for permission to revisit the tunnel via Denton House during June, as a result of which important photographic and video scenes were added to the collection.

## Condition of Tunnel in 1994

The condition of the tunnel structure varies greatly from place to place. Generally, the condition of the RSJs and galvanised corrugated iron sheets is good; in some places, it is excellent. The value of heavy galvanising is demonstrated beyond argument. Where non-galvanised corrugated iron was used, for example in the walls of the western exit gallery, it has decomposed to dust.

The worst deterioration of the tunnel lining is apparent for five yards at the western entrance immediately inside the outer gate where atmospheric contaminants from vehicular traffic on the adjacent road, and salt spray, borne by the prevailing winds have attacked the galvanised sheeting which is visibly corroded. The tunnel at this point additionally has solid brick walls with doubled RSJs and a concrete roof, built to resist military attack.

The adjacent guardroom was an early casualty to corrosion. It was apparently given an non-galvanised iron ceiling resulting in the chalk fall visible in the 1964 photographs which had existed for many years before. This is confirmed by the consolidation of the chalk by the scamper of many feet and the fact that the entrance had not been visited since it was last sealed. A Newhaven policeman assures me the chalk fall still existed in 1968 when he attended an incident. It appears it was removed, and the guardroom doorway blocked, to facilitate the consolidation work.

## Photographic Recording

Every opportunity was taken to photograph every facet of interest whilst access to the tunnel was available. This included colour prints, colour slides, and hours of video taken by different people. The outcome is a variety of pictures from which the best will be selected for exhibition as a permanent feature, for a slide show, and a companion video to this book.

Condensation was a great problem encountered on account of the high humidity and relatively high temperatures in the tunnel compared to the January near-freezing external temperatures to which everything was exposed before descent.

The photographic techniques employed were rather different to standard photography, because of the unusual dimensions and total darkness of the subject. It was found impossible to adequately floodlight even one gallery at a time; our cables were inadequate to carry the required power over the distances involved. However, the total darkness and absence of other persons enabled more specialised photographic techniques to be exploited.

These techniques involved placing the camera on a tripod and opening the lens, as for a time exposure of indefinite duration, whilst other functions were carefully performed in front of the lens. In one instance a second person fired a flashgun in the vicinity of the camera, and then repeatedly from concealed niches at ever increasing distances from the camera, making multiple exposures on one frame. In another instance the second person fired the flashgun in the vicinity of the camera, and then walked the length of the gallery carrying a lantern which was shielded from the camera's view by his body. The camera sees only the illuminated sides of the gallery; the silhouette cast by the lamp carrier was overwritten as he meandered from side to side illuminating the tunnel walls.

Both techniques require strict adherence to agreed procedures and verbal signals in total darkness. The results are staggering. The galleries appear to be fully and intensively floodlit, although in actual fact the lighting was momentary and the picture was built up over a minute or two. Wide-angle lenses were employed extensively to increase the feeling of presence, and on account of the confined spaces so often encountered. Light reflection varied dramatically and proved the greatest obstacle to successful results.

*West tunnel entrance 1964. The sentry house ceiling has collapsed spilling chalk through the doorway onto the flagstone floor. The sentry house firing port covered the entrance, and the curve provided visual and assault security.*
(Geoffrey Ellis, June 1964; © 1996)

*Plan of tunnel. Operations area.*   (Geoffrey Ellis, 20 December 1995)

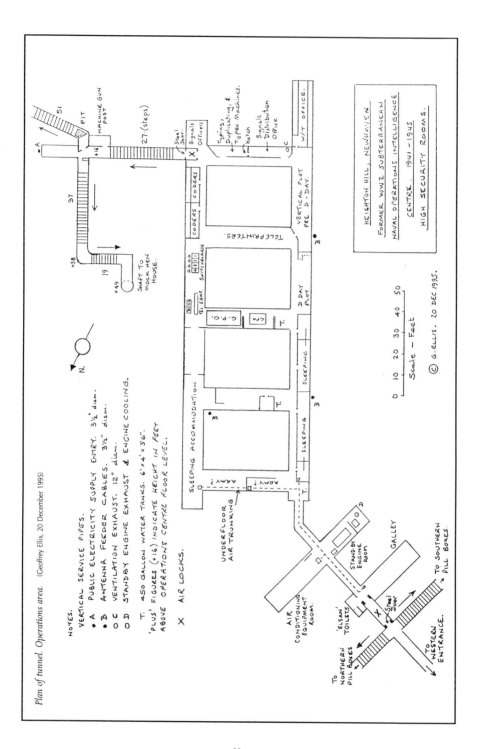

# EQUIPMENT INSTALLED AT HMS FORWARD

Since nothing now remains of the technical equipment once used in the tunnel, it is necessary to consider carefully what does survive by way of scant official archives, recollections of veterans who served here, and some fundamental facts, to provide an appreciation of the establishment and how it operated. This chapter might well have been titled 'Considering the evidence . . . '.

It is recorded that in 1942 the tunnel specifically contained . . .

(a) terminal equipment for telephone lines to ten RDF stations which feed both the Naval and Canadian Corps Coastal Artillery Plots. The Combined Headquarters of the Newhaven Sub-command and the Corps Coastal Artillery are situated in the tunnel beneath the Naval Headquarters. The information from the RDF stations feeding the Newhaven plot is essential to the Commander-in-Chief Portsmouth and to some extent the Vice-Admiral Dover. Both these authorities rely upon obtaining this information from NOIC's Headquarters.

(b) in addition to the above, the following telephone and communications are installed at Naval Headquarters:

Switchboards for Coastal Forces Base and local Naval telephones.
Terminal equipment for telephone lines to
C-in-C Portsmouth
Vice Admiral Dover
RAF Uxbridge
Various Army Units in Canadian Corps area including Corps HQ
Resident Naval Officer Shoreham
Resident Naval Officer Littlehampton
HMS VERNON (Roedean Girls School)
HMS NEWT (Newhaven — west side)
HMS LIZARD (to come)
Beachy Head Signals station

(c) terminal equipment of three four-channel teleprinter systems.

(d) terminal equipment of telephone control lines of Corps Coastal Artillery and teleprinter.

(e) W/T station of seven transmitting and receiving sets. This number to be increased and control lines to additional distant sets to be fitted.

(f) Telephone lines to control posts from QL and SF sites in the neighbourhood of Newhaven. The reference in (c) to 'three four-channel teleprinter systems' clearly dates this listing to April–June, 1942, (see later); the QL site probably refers to the harbour decoy provided at Exceat; and the SF site, the Special Fire equipment on Newhaven's east beach provided to set the sea ablaze in the event of invasion.

## The Air-conditioning Equipment

Well-informed looters relieved the deserted labyrinth of its rich source of wood and electrical items which were virtually unobtainable after the war. The ventilation plant, having less appeal, did not suffer to the same extent and much of it remains intact and in situ, although curiously, little air trunking survived in the long gallery nearest Denton House.

The ventilation system design features can be replicated easily and close inspection reveals how the air was distributed to the various galleries. The statistics required to calculate the volume of air contained in the operational centre served by ventilation system were provided by the detailed survey. Since some 1264 cubic metres of chalk was excavated from this area, it follows that the void contains 1,264,000 litres of air. A ventilation specialist could determine the size of the fan needed to produce (say) six changes of air per hour, and the power of the electrical heater required to maintain the quoted 65° Fahrenheit (18°C).

The operations centre was contained between two air-locks. The outer door of both airlocks were 5ft 8ins x 2ft 8ins x ⅝ins (1·727 x 0·812 x 0·016m) thick armour plate steel, weighed over 3cwt (150Kg) each, and closed onto a thick neoprene rubber seal. The inner doors, though less substantial, would have been strong enough to withstand the air pressure differential and would also have closed onto rubber seals.

The east end air-lock was used only by personnel to reach surface level within Denton House by climbing 122 steps in three flights. The west end air-lock was made longer (about 18ft — 5·5m) than the east end (about 6ft — 1·8m) to accommodate equipment and plant items which needed to enter or leave the operational area.

The west end air-lock additionally contained ventilation ducting, the orifices of which can be seen when facing the outside of the air-lock. Fresh air was drawn in from this point by the 12ins x 25ins (300 x 630mm) duct at the lower left. A 12ins x 10ins (300 x 250mm) duct above the fresh air inlet exhausted excess air once the desired pressure had been attained within the operational area. Another 7ins x 21ins (175 x 525mm) duct on the right hand side provided an independent air feed to the engine room annexe for engine cooling, to avoid decompression problems arising when the engine was running.

Fresh air was drawn into the ventilation system via a manually operated valve within the air-lock which could be closed in the event of a gas attack (access hatches in the trunking facilitated decontamination if necessary). Another valve in the fan room which normally mixed some internal air with the incoming fresh air, would then have been fully opened for total recirculation of the contained air.

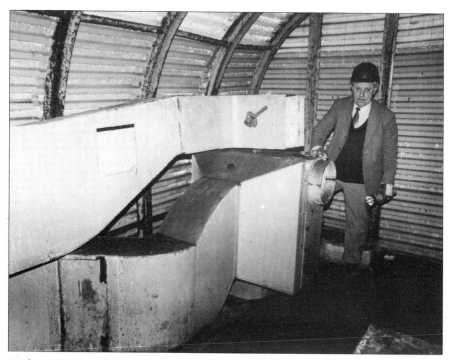

*Ventilation room. Air-conditioning trunking, filters and control valves.*

(Tom Bonnor, 1993)

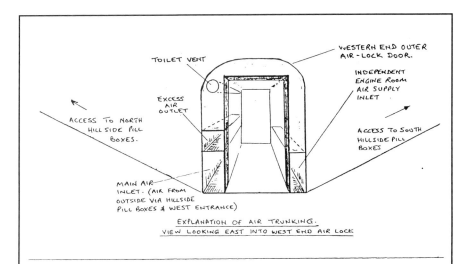

TOILET VENT

WESTERN END OUTER AIR-LOCK DOOR.

INDEPENDENT ENGINE ROOM AIR SUPPLY INLET

EXCESS AIR OUTLET

ACCESS TO NORTH HILLSIDE PILL BOXES.

ACCESS TO SOUTH HILLSIDE PILL BOXES

MAIN AIR INLET. (AIR FROM OUTSIDE VIA HILLSIDE PILL BOXES & WEST ENTRANCE)

EXPLANATION OF AIR TRUNKING.
VIEW LOOKING EAST INTO WEST END AIR LOCK

SIMPLIFIED EXPLANATION OF AIR DUCTING IN FAN ROOM.

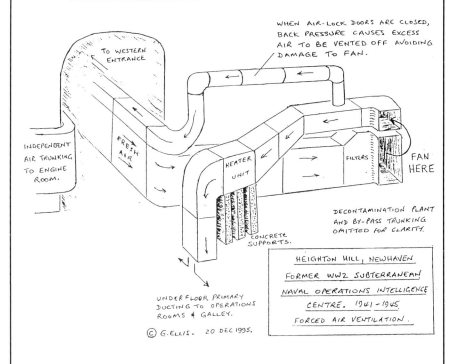

TO WESTERN ENTRANCE.

WHEN AIR-LOCK DOORS ARE CLOSED, BACK PRESSURE CAUSES EXCESS AIR TO BE VENTED OFF AVOIDING DAMAGE TO FAN.

INDEPENDENT AIR TRUNKING TO ENGINE ROOM.

FRESH AIR

HEATER UNIT

FILTERS

FAN HERE

DECONTAMINATION PLANT AND BY-PASS TRUNKING OMITTED FOR CLARITY.

CONCRETE SUPPORTS.

UNDERFLOOR PRIMARY DUCTING TO OPERATIONS ROOMS & GALLEY.

© G.ELLIS. 20 DEC 1995.

HEIGHTON HILL, NEWHAVEN
FORMER WW2 SUBTERRANEAN
NAVAL OPERATIONS INTELLIGENCE
CENTRE. 1941-1945
FORCED AIR VENTILATION.

*Ventilation room. Explanatory air flow.* (Geoffrey Ellis, 20 December 1995)

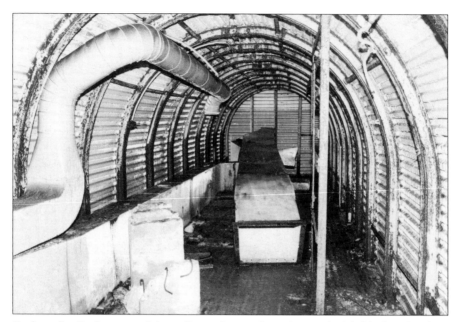

*Ventilation plant. Trunking seen toppled originally sat on lower trunking and connected with high level round trunking.*
(Geoffrey Ellis, 18 January 1993)

The incoming air next passed through a bank of filters to remove insects and dust particles, and was impelled into a decontamination unit which, in the event of a gas attack, would have 'washed' the air in a fine mist of water spray. (Storage tanks contained some 1350 gallons (4500l) of water against water supply failure). The cleaned air then passed into a chamber which vented off any excess pressure. The remaining air passed through an electric heater supported on reinforced concrete pillars into a cement lined underfloor duct leading to the Operations galleries and the galley where it emerged at 65° Fahrenheit. Today, the fan, the decontamination unit, and the heater have gone, but evidence of their existence is retained in the remaining trunking and reinforced concrete stanchions.

The metal frame in the fan room carried electrical switchgear, fuse boxes, meters, etc. Sadly, nothing now remains save signs of cable troughing in the floor leading to the engine room.

Ventilation requires a through draught. To facilitate air circulation, all partition walls contained hatches about 9ins (225mm) square covered with perforated zinc on both sides. Few door frames had doors. Stale air was collected in other trunking and expelled from the operations centre by exhaust trunking in the SDO and an extractor fan in the eastern air-lock venting the foul air outside through large diameter pipes.

## Stand-by Emergency Generator

The Operations Centre contained an emergency generator comprising a diesel engine and an alternator bolted to a concrete plinth measuring 9ft 2ins x 4ft x 7ins (2·8 x 1·22 x 0·175m) with ten vibration-absorbing rubber mountings which are still pliable. Marks on the wall and floor in the north-west corner of the room indicate the location of the engine control cubicle.

Few other artifacts remain except for one short length of iron pipe which starts about elbow level and follows the shape of the roof of the tunnel to a point above the engine, with a manifold type flange at the lower end. A large wooden block on the wall adjacent to the pipe reveals the former

*Emergency Generator room showing engine bed, independent cooling air duct, and doorway to annexe. Note curved pipe from former fuel pump to overhead fuel tank.*

(Geoffrey Ellis, 18 January 1993)

*Engine room annexe showing plinth for radiator and electric fan with cooling air supply duct. Len Miller on right.*

(Geoffrey Ellis, 25 January 1993)

existence of a hand-pump to fill the engine-mounted fuel tank, accounting for the manifold type flange on the pipe. There was no bulk fuel storage in the tunnel; fuel was brought into the engine room in large drums and hand-pumped as required into the small gravity feed tank above the engine.

The engine room had an annex approximately 9ft x 8ft 3ins (2.74 x 2.5m) containing a reinforced concrete plinth measuring 3ft x 2ft 6ins x 1ft 4ins high (0.915 x 0.76 x 0.406m) on which stood the engine radiator and its electric fan. The fan forced cold air from the independent air duct through the engine radiator and exhausted it through a special shaft avoiding decompressing the operational area.

A 10.5ins (266mm) diameter lined vertical shaft penetrates the ceiling of this annexe. It once reached the surface but is now blocked off near the top. This shaft also contained the 4ins (100mm) diameter engine exhaust pipe. The annex contained the engine starter battery — a dozen glass-sided lead acid cells sitting on a stout wooden battery rack. Fragments of an old sulphuric acid carbuoy, the remains of its strip metal basket, and a tuft of straw were found here.

Nothing tangible remains to determine the exact rating of the alternator. An inspired guess, based upon estimates of lighting and equipment loading under operational conditions, and the size of the engine exhaust pipe, suggests it would not have been less than 20kVA, and may have been as high as 50kVA. The emergency generator would have been routinely used during surface air raids to avoid interruptions to operations due to public electricity supply failure caused by enemy action.

Battery powered emergency lighting would have provided short-term minimal illumination for evacuation purposes in the event of failure of the public electricity supply and a catastrophe to the stand-by generator. Such a scenario could have been possible if the engine exhaust had been damaged by bomb or direct enemy action.

## The Wireless Telegraphy Office

The W/T Office was situated at the south end of the western long gallery close to the Signals Distribution Office.

*The W/T Office, the entrance was in foreground, left of the fallen air trunking. This breeze-block partition was totally destroyed. The painted white oblong on floor marks the location of a stationery cupboard.*

(Geoffrey Ellis, 15 June 1994)

RN Leading Telegraphist Victor Sievey who served with HMS FORWARD from May to October, 1944, and who still retains his interest in radio communication as a licensed radio amateur (G4PTC/RNAS 3873) recalls there were seven Marconi CR100 receivers and transmitting keys on the left of the room; and two Eddystone 358 and two National HRO receivers on the right of the room with 'a battery of intercom phones' between them. The regular transmitters were off-site but stand-by transmitters existed elsewhere in the complex.

## Telephones and Telephone Switchboards

During the war years, Newhaven had a CBS2 (Central Battery Signalling) manual telephone exchange which stood on the site now (1996) occupied by the Post Office. The CBS2 public telephone exchange did not supply current to operate the transmitters (microphones) of the telephones as today's exchanges do. Each and every telephone on the system had a separate local battery to supply this power whether it was an exchange line, or extension. This was normally supplied by three series-connected primary cells (DR2 or R30) contained in a wooden battery box. Remnants of many such battery boxes have been found in the tunnel.

Technical drawings discovered specify the use of Bellsets 25; Instruments, Telephone 246; and Units Auxiliary Apparatus N 1616 on the extensions. Two former GPO telephone engineers recall the provision of secrecy (scrambler) equipment in the Guinness Trust Home and in the tunnel. Scramblers were used on certain extensions to prevent casual or accidental (or clandestine) overhearing of sensitive information. These were electronic devices which distorted speech beyond recognition by inverting the voice frequencies sent down the telephone line. A scrambler telephone was required at each end of a line, and usually had a green handset.

In the entombed void beneath room 16, four short lengths of lead covered telephone cables were discovered. Two were 20-pair lacquered and waxed double cotton covered switchboard cables; one was a 15-pair lacquered and paper insulated cable. The fourth was a 54-pair (quad) cable commonly used for trunk circuits with lacquered conductors and paper insulation. They had been built into the brickwork when the tunnel was sealed, and had been sawn off when it later proved impossible to recover them. The 15-pair cable contained a neatly plumbed joint; the varnished wires had been cleaned and soldered, carefully sleeved, and cocooned in waxed paper before the cable sheath was expertly plumbed up.

The two 20-pair cables could have served up to forty extension telephones within Denton House; veteran GPO telephone engineer Dennis Tompsett spoke of "a Despatch Office adjacent to Denton House main entrance with a dozen telephones, and many others in rooms used as offices". The other cables could have carried up to sixty-nine 'external' circuits to more distant destinations.

There were many external extensions and private wires to other service establishments not officially recorded; RAF Friston — a 'Forward Landing Ground', RAF Benson, RAF Ford, and RAF Tangmere.

Telephone circuits to remote destinations left the tunnel by both exits for network security. Cables routed via Denton House left via the east wing in two earthenware ducts which led from the machinery store beneath room 4 to Heighton Road.

Very little remained in Denton House to suggest the Military was here at all, apart from the commemorative plaque above the fireplace, some abandoned pneumatic tubing in the loft and two short lengths of Don-8 wire alongside it. (Don-8 wire was used extensively by the army along hedgerows for field telephones. It consisted of one tinned copper wire and seven tinned iron strands with rubber insulation covered by wax impregnated jute braid. It was very hard wearing, and as this sample proves, very durable).

Dennis Tompsett recalls that initially there was a two-position doll's eye switchboard (probably 10+50 type) in the tunnel. This was succeeded by a four-position PMBX1A (Private Manual Branch Exchange No. 1A) which served the tunnel, the Headquarters, and various external extensions. Documentation discovered refers to extensions 11 & 12 being used for Air/Sea rescue coordination. These extension numbers were not proper to the later switchboard; Air/Sea rescue was performed here in 1942, but had been transferred to Newhaven by 1943.

*Most northerly interconnecting tunnel. Possibly used for Army CCC Battalion HQ. View looking East.*

(Geoffrey Ellis, 15 June 1994)

*Most northerly interconnecting tunnel. Possibly used for Army CCC Battalion HQ. View looking west. This is the same gallery and view as IWM H14504 taken during excavation (see page 61).*

(Geoffrey Ellis, 15 June 1994)

WRNS switchboard operators say the switchboard was changed (both in type and location) towards the end of 1943. The new PMBX1A was installed in the eastern large gallery close to the interconnecting gallery which accommodated the teleprinters. From some remarks about 'being able to see into the teleprinter office from the leftmost switchboard position' it is possible to pinpoint the exact location of this suite of switchboards. To the right of the switchboards were some equipment racks and tucked away behind them was a bunk bed for rest periods during night watches.

PMBX1A telephone switchboards need a 50 volt negative supply of perhaps 50AH capacity to operate their signalling lamps, relays, and a ringing current generator; and a smaller 50 volt positive supply as well. These requirements are normally supplied by racks of secondary cells, but the location of these batteries has not been determined. Following recovery from the tunnel in 1945, two of these PMBX1A switchboards were reinstalled in the Grand Hotel, and another in the Burlington Hotel, at Eastbourne where they remained in service until the mid 1980s.

The Canadian Coastal Corps Battalion Headquarters had a separate 10+50 PBX (a manual switchboard catering for up to ten exchange lines and fifty extensions). They had their own network of circuits to Army coastal radar stations, outposts and Gun Operations Centres, and their administrative HQ situated in the Manor House, Denton.

## Teleprinters

GPO Telephones provided and maintained the Creed 7B teleprinters which stood on DTN (Defence Teleprinter Network) type tables made specially to accommodate all the equipment needed to create a teleprinter workstation, i.e. a customised metal desk complete with plugs, sockets, and power units. Similar tables may be seen in the tunnels at Hellfire Corner, beneath Dover Castle.

The teleprinter room retained its identity throughout the life of the establishment. Whilst initially there were only three operational teleprinters, by D-Day there were eight Naval teleprinters plus one used by the Army, and another provided in the GPO VF terminal for testing purposes.

## Telegraph Terminal Equipment.

Where teleprinters are used over distances of more than a few miles, the teleprinter signals must be converted into tones which are easier to send down a telephone line, (and be amplified on the way if necessary). The tones are then reconverted back to teleprinter signals again at the far end. The equipment to do this is known as Voice Frequency Telegraph Terminal Equipment. Four similar equipments were mounted on a standard telephone apparatus rack which stood 8ft 6.5ins (2.6m) high. Since the maximum height of the tunnel is 8ft (2.4m), the floor level had to be lowered by almost 2ft (0.6m) to allow for overhead air trunking and cabling; hence the curious pits in the central gallery floor.

One pit is 14ft 11ins long, 2ft deep and 6ft 6ins wide at floor level (4.5 x 0.6 x 1.98m) with 'dripping pan' sides reducing to 4ft 10ins (1.47m) at the bottom. In one corner there is a step. When cleared of rubbish and 700 gallons of water, the floor of this pit revealed rawlplug marks where four 20ins-wide Voice Frequency Telegraph equipment racks had once stood side by side. Curiously, three racks appear not to have been fixed to the floor.

In an adjacent room, then beyond a breeze-block partition, is another pit for a similar reason. This pit measures 7ft 6ins long, 2ft deep and 6ft 6ins wide (2.3 x 0.61 x 1.98m) with vertical sides edged with angle iron. This pit appears to have accommodated two racks of similar VF telegraph terminal equipment and an MDF (Main Distribution Frame). An MDF is simply an iron frame carrying terminal strips and fuse mountings on which all internal and external cables are terminated, together with cabling to all the equipment to which those cables may need to be connected, including local telephone distribution cables, VF terminal equipment, switchboard equipment, and teleprinter equipment. It is then an easy matter to connect anything to anything with a short piece of expendable wire which may be easily rearranged if necessary, quickly and cheaply. It is a primary flexibility point and every public telephone exchange has one in some form or another.

Documentary evidence reveals that one four-channel teleprinter terminal rack installed at

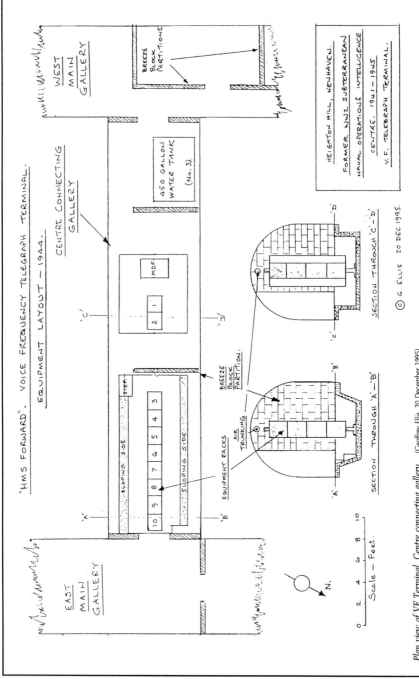

*Plan view of VF Terminal. Centre connecting gallery.* (Geoffrey Ellis, 20 December 1995)

Newhaven Fort in May, 1940, was recovered in January, 1942, to be reinstalled in the tunnel with a second identical equipment. This provided an initial capacity for eight channels (circuits). Three months later a third rack was added. Could this have been provision for the Dieppe raid, originally planned for April, 1942, but ultimately postponed? Another rack was added, probably in June/July ready for the eventual Dieppe raid on 19 August, 1942. This doubled the capacity to sixteen channels.

In September, 1943, the installation was extended by five racks transferred from Amport House (Air Ministry Station) in Andover. In hindsight this can be interpreted as augmenting the communications infrastructure for the forthcoming Normandy landings. The installation now provided capacity for thirty-six teleprinter channels.

Not all of this capacity was used by the Navy. It is known that one teleprinter circuit served Lewes Road Barracks at Brighton, and another served the Canadian Corps Coastal Artillery HQ. Where essential circuits are involved, it is customary to provide alternative routings for immediate use in case of emergency. This necessitates idle plant being allocated and available for immediate use; doubtless some of this capacity was dedicated to this purpose.

## Cryptographic Equipment

A Wren Coder recalls Typex machines in the office adjacent to the SDO with the Imperial Typewriter and Ormig duplicator. Presumably the keyboard skills required to operate Typex machines dictated their installation where these talents existed.

Typex machines resembled typewriters, but produced two thin paper tapes. When plain language was typed in, one tape contained the plain language copy for verification, the other contained the coded message in five letter groups. Alternatively, code typed in would produce copies of the code and the decoded message. This was the British version of the German Enigma machine, but much bigger, faster and noisier. These machines had many millions of code variations which changed with every character typed. Theoretically impossible to decipher without another machine and set-up instructions, the code from these machines certainly gave the enemy a bad time. By the time any code had been broken the message content would have been history.

## Lamson Paragon pneumatic message carrier

Approximately 200ft (61m) of pneumatic message tube exists from the operational area, up the stairs towards Denton House to where it was dismantled to build the wall. Lengths of tube (a straight section and a short curve) and a hole in the breeze-block wall at high level reveal where the tube entered the Signals Distribution Office. This has since been confirmed by a former SDO occupant.

In Denton House roof another 110ft (33m) of tubing was discovered running through the West wing loft between Room 16 and the beginning of the first floor loft where it was dismantled to facilitate the installation of some modern central heating plumbing. The Denton House end originally terminated in the Dispatch office close to the main door.

The pneumatic message carrier comprised a hollow cylindrical 'holder' made from compressed fibre (not unlike a torch handle) with soft leather covered brass end caps which twisted to reveal the cavity within the device into which a message could be placed, and then twisted again to retain it. The carrier was placed into a breach at one end of the 2·125ins (54mm) pneumatic tube to be propelled by vacuum (or air pressure) to the distant end where it was ejected into a wire basket with great commotion. Such devices were once common in departmental stores when a single cashier handled all the cash transactions.

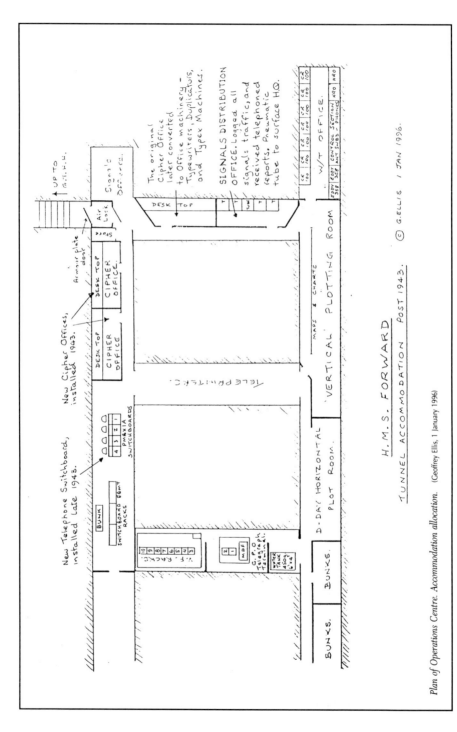

*Plan of Operations Centre. Accommodation allocation.* (Geoffrey Ellis, 1 January 1996)

UP TO G.P.O.

Signals Office.

Air Lock

Store

Armour plate door

DESK TOP

CIPHER OFFICE.

New Cipher Offices, installed 1943.

DESK TOP

CIPHER OFFICE.

New Telephone Switchboard, installed late 1943.

PMBX1A SWITCHBOARDS

4 3 2 1

BUNK

SWITCHBOARD EQPT RACKS

V.F. RACKS.

10 9 8 7 6 5 4 3 2 1

G.P.O. Telegraph Terminal

M.D.F.

2 1

WATER TANK 4500 GALS

TELEPRINTERS

The original Cipher Office later converted to Office machinery – Typewriters, Duplicators, and Typex Machines.

SIGNALS DISTRIBUTION OFFICE. Logged all signals traffic, and received telephoned reports. Pneumatic tube to surface H.Q.

DESK TOP

T T T T

W/T OFFICE.

CR 100 | CR 100 | CR 100 | CR 100 | CR 100

EBY DSP ANT SUBS PHONES

CONTROL STATION

WRO

WRO

MAPS & CHARTS

'VERTICAL' PLOTTING ROOM

D-DAY HORIZONTAL PLOT ROOM.

BUNKS.

BUNKS.

H.M.S. FORWARD

TUNNEL ACCOMMODATION POST 1943.

© G. ELLIS 1 JAN 1996.

# OFFICES & DUTIES

HMS FORWARD collected, processed, and distributed maritime intelligence, both friendly and hostile, concerning a section of the English Channel from Fairlight near Hastings, to Bognor Regis. The Canadian Corps Coastal Artillery had a HQ here and shared this information. This chapter reveals how and where that intelligence was processed and what is known of the roles and duties performed in the various offices which have been positively identified.

Few clues remain today which reveal the use of galleries other than those used for the air-conditioning plant, stand-by generator and telegraph terminal. Looters destroyed any residual visible evidence whilst salvaging wood battening, and the only resource remaining today is the memories of surviving veterans who served here during the war. In those days they were positively discouraged, even forbidden, to visit any area of the tunnel other than their specific domain. I am therefore indebted to all the veterans who have come forward to volunteer information concerning their sphere of activity, revealing the full picture.

It is now clear that the establishment evolved during the course of the war to meet changing scenarios. Evidence of this is to be found in the developing Telegraph VF terminal, the new cipher offices, the new larger switchboard, and relocated galley. Some early ships crew had difficulty reconciling their memories with the final drawings because 'it was not like that in their days.'

The following paragraphs describe the organisation, operation, development, and importance of the subterranean intelligence centre and its connections with the world outside as revealed by the veterans who served here.

## Naval Officers-in-Charge, HMS FORWARD

The following Officers commanded HMS FORWARD.
Captain A A Lovett-Cameron RN (1942)
Admiral Hardman-Jones (1942–44)
Vice-Admiral R V Halt (1944)
Vice-Admiral Sir T J Hallett (1944–45)
The tunnel was commanded by Col. Cheeseman RM (Retd), who stood over 6ft (1·8m) tall. He is described as a typical Royal Marine Officer, a confirmed and dedicated military disciplinarian. He was forced to duck his head whilst walking in the access galleries and could only stand erect in the major galleries where the additional headroom was not obstructed by light fittings, or air ducting. When a heart condition prevented him from climbing stairs he used a staff car to gain access via the western entrance. He (and a number of my correspondents) spent some time in the RN Sick Bay.

## The Signals Distribution office

All signals and messages received by W/T, teleprinter, telephone, or messenger were logged and typed up in the SDO and forwarded by the most appropriate means. Within the tunnel, documents were passed by messengers, but a pneumatic message tube was used to convey small documents to the Despatch Office near the front door of the Guinness Trust Holiday Home where the messages would be delivered (internally) by messenger, or consigned externally by WRNS Despatch Riders on motorcycles.

WRNS Nancy Longstaff (now Thompson) responded to my appeals for assistance from her home in Ormond Beach, Florida. She told me:

*"I went to the tunnel in Denton as a nineteen year old Signals Wren from February, 1944, to July, 1945, working in the Signals Distribution Office. We had a long bench against the tunnel wall with four telephones and a message 'tube' in the middle between them. There*

*Picture of Col Cheeseman & Heirarchy. 1942.*

(Newhaven Local & Maritime Museum, 1942)

*was a small hatchway into an adjacent office with an old Imperial typewriter and an Ormig spirit duplicating machine.*

*"I was on night watch when the Landing Craft went to Normandy, 5/6 June, 1944; we had ATS and WAAF girls working down there. I lived with other Wrens in Surrey House, Seaford, and we were taken on duty by bus, and went into the Guinness Trust Holiday Home walking along a passage, then down the steps to our offices. The worst part was after a very hectic Duty Watch having to walk up about 120 steps. We went to a Nissen Hut for breakfast after night watch before the bus took us back to Seaford.*

*"The conditions were poor, no food provided, just facilities for making cups of tea. Young ones today wouldn't work like we did for little pay. Before I left in July, 1945, parties of girls who worked at the Harbour were given a tour of the tunnel and were appalled at what they saw. They apologised to us for nagging us about being off duty sometimes during the day forgetting that we worked unsociable hours and weekends, etc, as the tunnel never closed.*

*"Air/Sea Rescue messages to RAF Uxbridge went via our office as there was no teleprinter at the harbour. I often typed out the monthly list of rescues in the Channel — how many picked up, alive or dead, and nationality. On one occasion after a report of a plane ditched in a certain locality, the rescue launch fortuitously stumbled across three Americans in a dinghy which hadn't been reported.*

*"RN Signalmen who worked watches at the PWSS (Port War Signal Station) on the clifftop at the entrance to the harbour rang our office to report any vessels entering or leaving harbour. We didn't visit other offices in the tunnel, it just wasn't allowed. I seemed to sit at the Imperial typewriter continually during duty as the pile of messages waiting for me every watch was unbelievable."*

Nancy is quoted in Ursula Stuart Mason's book "Britannia's Daughters" describing her recollections of the eve of D-Day.

WRNS Violet Bedwell (now Coles), Telephonist, told me "We worked in the bowels of the

*The SDO (Signals Distribution Office) through which all signals passed and were recorded. Four telephones and the pneumatic message terminal stood on a bench against the tunnel wall. Note air exhaust with integral conduit on right.*

(Geoffrey Ellis, 15 June 1994)

*The SDO typing and duplicating room. Note service hatch from the SDO. There was Typex equipment here 1944. This was the cipher office 1942/43.*

(Geoffrey Ellis, 15 June 1994)

earth in a tunnel; two offices, a partition between, a typist on one side and I on the other. The signals were checked, some were very long especially the meteorological reports. Some messages were telephoned in from outlying posts by the coastguards, as everything entering or leaving the harbour had to be notified, but most messages came from the teleprinters. When the messages had been typed and duplicated, I had to distribute the copies as necessary".

WRNS Peggy Matthews (now Bentley) records "In the SDO there were six personnel to a watch — one Petty Officer, two Leading Hands, and three WRNS ratings. There were three watches per day with equal numbers of persons on duty at all times. From March until September, 1944, there was no leave because of pressure of work".

## The Despatch Office

This was an office just inside the main door of the Guinness Trust Holiday Home with a pneumatic message tube communicating with the Signals Distribution Office in the tunnel. WRNS Despatch Riders conveyed messages telegraphed via HMS FORWARD destined for outstationed shorebased 'ships' in the Sub-command. In-house communications were delivered by messenger.

## Cipher Office

The original cipher office location was the office adjacent to the SDO. It was clearly inadequate for the expected demands of the forthcoming invasion, because in late 1943 two timber-built offices were constructed near the stairs and SDO, in a long gallery formerly reported to have been used for sleeping accommodation. Today only painted white lines remain on the flagstones outlining an area 33ft x 6ft (10 x 1·8m) with two gaps suggesting entrances. WRNS Pauline Tipler, recalling her approach to the switchboards, first revealed this was the location of two cipher offices.

WRNS Joyce "Mitch" Mitchell (now Kitson) served here. Another former WRNS coder explained that one office was for WRNS ratings who coded normal traffic; the other was for WRNS Officers who coded highly sensitive and confidential signals, and personally delivered these messages to whom they were intended.

Messages transmitted or received by radio were always coded, as were most text messages transmitted and received by teleprinter over landline. WRNS cryptographers coded or decoded all incoming and outgoing traffic.

PRO documents indicate that a favoured form of coding was by use of the One Time Pad (OTP). A One Time Pad, as its name suggests was a cipher to be used once only, and then discarded. By using a different cipher for each message, the enemy was unable to crack our messages through repetition. Another system called AQUA is said to have been used briefly around D-Day.

## The Teleprinter Office

WRNS Betty Connell (now Storey) and Rene Beretta (now Peett) recalled eight teleprinters in two rows of four, back-to-back in the teleprinter room. Frequent plotting updates and other communications were exchanged by teleprinter to Dover, Portsmouth and London. After D-Day they often got through to ANCXF Paris. HMS FORWARD handled all signals for HMS AGGRESSIVE, HMS NEWT, and other shore-based ships in the sub-command which did not possess teleprinters. A typical duty watch comprised one Leading Wren, and five ordinary Wrens.

Rolls of abandoned manifold teleprinter paper indicate that duplicate carbon copies of all messages were produced.

## The Plotting Office

The plotting office was the nucleus of the centre. The plotting room map displayed all the culminated intelligence in a readily understandable form. In the true Naval tradition, the original map was vertical, but for D-Day there was a change to horizontal presentation.

Naval plots usually use geographical coordinates of latitude and longitude, but here it was more convenient to use National Grid References (extended to cover the Channel) to maintain uniformity with the Army and RAF whose procedures employed these parameters.

*The finished "Ops" room with WRNS at work on the telephones (Both Army and Navy would use the Control when completed).*
(© IWM; Photo H 14502, 2 October 1941)

Anything detected by radar going up, down, across, under, or over the Channel was reported to this office where information regarding the nature, quantity, direction, speed, and nationality of the report would be represented by a marker placed on a map of the English Channel indicating its whereabouts.

IWM photograph H14502 shows a group of WRNS & RN, with an army Officer at work in the finished 'OPs' room according to the legend. This location is adjacent to the SDO and shows the door to the W/T Office. The picture illustrates the importance of the telephone in this situation where almost everybody has their own instrument. There are many anomalies in this picture which reveal it was posed prematurely to pacify the Admiralty!

Major Tom K Hitchins TD RA (Retd) recalled "I was posted to HMS FORWARD in 1942 to set up a combined Army/Naval plotting room beneath Naval HQ. I drew the wall chart on which we plotted the movements of shipping moving east and west — our own Navy, and hostile shipping off the French coast. Sometimes we picked up E-boats and passed the information to Coastal Batteries who might fire off a round or two. We had a staff of twenty-four ATS and twenty-four WRNS as plotters and telephonists receiving reports from the CDCHL (Coastal Defence Chain Home Low) radar stations from Fairlight to Littlehampton, and we were in contact with Dover and Portsmouth Naval HQ who would identify the plots from their knowledge of ship movements. I was there at the time of the Dieppe Raid. I left this appointment after about six months". (Some years later when Tom Hitchins was promoted to Major, he returned to Newhaven and assumed command of Newhaven Fort. He was the last CO of the Fort and closed it down).

WRNS Plotter Trixie Williams (now Gell) served at HMS FORWARD from September, 1942, to 4 July, 1945, initially as a messenger. After three months of dashing up and down the 122 steps she was promoted to Plotter and really enjoyed it. Trixie told me "At the beginning we had two Wrens on Plotting duty, on a twenty-four-hour shift system. Then as things hotted up we had more and more personnel drafted in and we hardly had any space at all in the plotting room. There were RAF and

*Scene in the Plotting room at 0730 hrs on 6 June, 1944. Fourteen of the sixteen people (mixed rank, service, gender and nationality) endorsed this print, including the Commodore. Note the inverted fluorescent lights. The air trunking and doorway positively identify this location.*

(Geoffrey Ellis; © 1994)

*Location of the D-Day plotting room fifty years later, taken from the same point. This picture reveals the adjacent sleeping accommodation (part of the block partition is missing), and the passageway leading to the western entrance.*

(Geoffrey Ellis; © 1994).

*Chief Petty Officer "Nobby" Clark and Leading Hand Clasby opposite the western entrance with Tarring Neville in background.*

(Tom Bonnor; © 1993)

WAAFs as well with us at the end". This report is well supported by the priceless photograph which records for posterity the scene in the HMS FORWARD Plotting room at 0730hrs on D-Day, 6 June, 1944, where sixteen personnel of different rank, gender and military persuasion (RN, WRNS, RNVR, RCNVR, RAF, & WAAF) had spent the entire night watch. Trixie is seated at the plotting table to the left of the Commodore.

Fourteen of the sixteen people in the photograph endorsed this print. The picture was clearly taken with the Commodore's approval for he was not only looking at the camera, but also signed it. The photographer knew his business to get such a well-balanced picture with flash in such a restricted location, and was well aware that he was photographing a truly historic event. This is the only genuine operational photograph known to have been taken inside the tunnel during hostilities.

Trixie explained how the plot functioned. "Dover and Portsmouth exchanged plots with Newhaven at ten-minute intervals according to which way the convoys were proceeding. If there was a 'flap' on, U-boats about etc, they were sent and received more frequently. The plots we received from the RAF stations (Beachy Head, etc) were six figures and we had to quickly convert them into four figures by 'correcting' the second and fifth digits according to the value of the third and sixth digits. For example, 126899 would become 1390. Quite easy when you got the hang of it, but you maybe had several numbers to deal with because of stragglers and escorts etc.

"There was a small cabin on the top of Beachy Head where the RAF and WAAFs were using their Radar equipment. I had an exchange with a WAAF for a week and worked in the hut, but didn't understand one blip from another. At Newhaven we had to pass these plots on to Dover and Portsmouth.

"We worked an average of forty-four hours a week on four- and twelve-hour shifts, but when things hotted up we lost our days off. We might get a couple of hours sleep at nights according to the convoy movements, but if there was a force-ten gale, we could do our knitting as nothing ventured out. Twice, when our days off were cancelled, I landed up in Sick Bay with nervous exhaustion. The RN Sick Bay was Gracie Fields' former house in Dorothy Avenue, Peacehaven."

Masie Hill, WRNS Plotter, recorded her service with HMS FORWARD in August, 1944, in Ursula Stuart Mason's book "Britannia's Daughters."

The Plotters continued to work until there was no further threat from U-boats. On 4 July, 1945, all plotters were posted to HMS HERON at Yeovilton.

## The Wireless Telegraphy office

Victor Sievey, a Naval Leading Telegraphist who served with HMS FORWARD from May to October, 1944, stated that during this period the W/T office was to all intents and purposes run on a day-to-day basis by one CPO Tel First Class "Nobby" Clark, ably assisted by three-badge L/Tel Clasby. Two civilian gents who worked days only (day and day about) were Marconi operators working in a supervisory capacity for the War Office. Affectionately known as Uncle Alf and Uncle Stu, they were extremely good and efficient operators who had served on the cross-Channel boats and were well experienced in Channel radio working conditions.

Vic met his wife Betty Smith (now Sievey) whilst at Newhaven — she was a WRNS Telegraphist in the same office. I interviewed them when they returned to Denton House on the D-Day fiftieth anniversary Sunday, 5 June, 1994, with Cyril "Cigs" Taylor, another veteran RN Telegraphist.

Vic remembers HMS FORWARD callsign was MFF. The 500KHz International Distress Frequency was constantly monitored and also one of the coastguard frequencies (probably Niton Radio). A timed watch was also kept on Rugby W/T on a LF worldwide frequency.

The port of Newhaven was an MTB (Motor Torpedo Boat) base whose motto could have been 'Attack is the best method of Defence'. Enemy ports and shipping were their primary objectives. Many commendations were earned by the crews of these craft in the pursuit of their duties, and sadly, more than a few failed to return following an engagement. Once embarked on a mission their only contact was by radio to HMS FORWARD who plotted their progress and advised any compromising developments. A night watch was kept constantly on the frequency used by the MTBs going out from HMS AGGRESSIVE at the harbour. Night operations usually commenced with the boats going out at about 1800/1900hrs.

## Telephone Switchboards

Pauline Tipler, WRNS Switchboard Operator, who served at HMS FORWARD from January, 1944, to July, 1945, is blessed with a very retentive memory and keeps autograph and photograph albums which have established beyond doubt many facts which might never otherwise have been told. Pauline remembers that, as in the plotting room, the switchboard operators were joined by ATS and WAAF telephonists during the lead up to D-Day.

Whilst the Army had a switchboard and a teleprinter in their HQ here, the locations have not been determined as surviving Canadian Corps Army veterans have proved more difficult to find.

## Skills and Conditions

Many WRNS categories were involved with HMS FORWARD HQ including Coders, Drivers, Despatch Riders, Messengers, Plotters, Switchboard Operators, Telegraphists, Telephonists, Teleprinter Operators, Typists, Watchkeepers, and Writers. There were basically three 'watches' per day with a three week rota which involved consecutive watches and split watches, although not all duties followed the same pattern. Duties were further influenced by enemy action, military exercises, and the weather.

WRNS were paid according to their category, a messenger receiving 16s/0d (80p) per week, and a typist receiving £1/4s (£1·20) per week, paid fortnightly. Pay parades were held in the Guinness Trust Home, and RN and WRNS alike had to parade before the HMS FORWARD Paymaster and salute before receiving their dues.

It is impossible to establish exact staffing levels, which would have been subject to considerable variation anyway during the life of the tunnel. The early report by Major Tom Hitchens that 'forty-eight ATS & WRNS plotters and telephonists' served in the plotting room apparently takes no account of the SDO, W/T, Coders, Teleprinter or Switchboard Operators and other personnel outside his jurisdiction. Staff increased dramatically during 1943, peaking with D-Day when up to a hundred were on duty on each watch, and diminishing after September, 1944, until July, 1945, when the remaining WRNS were posted elsewhere and the HQ closed down.

# MISCELLANEOUS ANECDOTES

This chapter includes a selection of interesting anecdotes related by veterans who served in the tunnel. Some are amusing, others more factual, but all illustrate the wartime atmosphere and add a personal element to this establishment.

Len Miller, General Post Office Telephone Engineer and Linesman for Newhaven Telephone Exchange, whose duties included the maintenance of the telephone and telegraph equipment in the tunnel, remembers the German battleships Scharnhorst, Gneiseneau & Prinz Eugen sailing up Channel on 11 February, 1942. He vividly described that particular evening, recalling his experiences as though they had happened the day before.

"I was asked to come up here one day urgently to put on some more circuits between Newhaven and Dover. The reason for it was that radar equipment between Bournemouth and Poole had spotted two large unidentified targets proceeding up the channel in very bad weather. So big were these targets that they were assumed to be major battleships; but the powers that be thought the equipment was faulty. They couldn't possibly be coming up there at that time, but eventually we found out that they were, and they were passing up the channel. Obviously a lot of people wanted to know about it, and I was sent up here to do the work.

"I approached the Guinness Trust House at the top of the hill. There was a bristle of machine guns and people rushing around and general pandemonium reigned, so I thought I won't bother to go in there, whatever they're doing, (I thought it was an exercise), so I went down to the Lewes road and came in the bottom entrance where the guard on duty knew me quite well. I went in and started to get on with my work. Then Col Cheeseman came along and wanted to know what I was doing in here, and I told him. So he said 'Well, I didn't call for you.' So I said 'Well no, I didn't speak to you, but I understand it was on your instructions that I'm here,' but he wouldn't agree to it and locked me up because they didn't think I was supposed to be in here. I can only assume that they thought I was doing things I shouldn't be doing. But anyway they then realised that they weren't getting these circuits that they'd asked for, and they came and saw me then, and I said 'Well no — that's what I was doing and you locked me up and stopped me doing it. Until you let me out, you'll have to wait for the circuits.' Then it was agreed that I could carry on with my job."

This was the first significant occurrence since the tunnel became operational, and it could not have been better placed to report on this particular situation.

Later, standing near the pits in the VF Telegraph terminal, Len recalled: "Through the centre here was racks of Voice Frequency Telegraph Equipment. The reason the holes are here, is because the racks of equipment were too high, so they had to sink the cement floor.

"The Navy, being bitten with cleanliness, there was always people sweeping up, and clearing up, and tidying up and painting all the time. Every time the chap came around here with the broom he created dust which put our equipment out of order. So I got hold of Col Cheeseman in charge of this place and asked if they could either stop cleaning in here, because they were doing more harm than good, or get some linoleum on the floor to keep the dust down. He got hold of one of my bosses — I never heard the conversation but I don't think he got the linoleum — but a week later that linoleum arrived. I think it's of Admiralty extraction; it was put down here and it stopped a lot of the trouble."

Another Newhaven GPO Telephone Engineer, Dennis Tompsett was here when the tunnel was being was being built and equipped. Standing in the central interconnecting gallery where the larger of two shallow pits were excavated he recalled "This area was the first area which was opened up to give enough height for the racks of equipment. Initially it started with three racks, and the builder who had dug it out and plastered the sides had just finished.

"The Col came down with me and said to the chap "You've done a very good job here but I've got news for you, we're going to extend it, so you're going to have to knock it down and enlarge it." That poor guy, I thought he was going to drop dead on the spot because it was pretty tough work digging around here then re-bricking it and plastering it. But as you can see it gradually grew until it got to this size."

Miss Pauline Tipler served as a WRNS Switchboard Operator in the tunnel from January, 1944, to July, 1945. Pauline's retentive memory and retained memorabilia have been most helpful in establishing the uses of the main galleries. Her autograph album has many entries for 'the last night in the tunnel' by Wrens who were being dispersed to other Naval establishments the next day. They are all signed 'Tunnel Rats' and dated 29 June, 1945 (Friday).

Pauline recalls: "On 18 March, 1944, we were inspected by HRH Duchess of Kent (Princess Marina) — a lovely personality who spoke to as many of us on Parade as was possible in the time. (We greatly admired her black silk stockings)."

WRNS Telegraphist Marguerite Humphreys (now Curtis) arrived at HMS FORWARD after the visit by the Duchess of Kent, but was there for the visit by Dame Vera Laughton-Matthews (Head of the WRNS). Marguerite particularly remembers Lieut Bruce-Lockhart who is prominent in the tunnel D-Day photograph, because he had a languid air of confidence and was noted for wearing blue silk pyjamas showing from under his uniform if called to the tunnel at night.

Marguerite was on watch on VE Day and received the following message . . . "NE v PO, QPM SN581, OP-A-AVC 081500B UA SPLICE THE MAINBRACE, by Buzzer, 0322, 8/5". That evening, she says, "a gang of us went to Brighton and sang and danced in the streets".

WRNS Nancy Longstaff (now Thompson) and Peggy Matthews (now Bentley) recalled one poignant incident which occurred whilst a certain ATS girl was serving in the tunnel. In the course of their Signals Distribution Office duties they had to log all teleprinter messages; date, time, content, etc. On this occasion, information arrived concerning the crew of an MTB blown up at Ostende. A Petty Officer aboard that MTB was the husband of the ATS lass, and he had been killed. The Navy didn't tell her until three days later. It was awful, they said, that they knew and she didn't. They kept asking each other "Has she said anything yet?"

RN L/Telegraphist Vic Sievey (who served in the W/T office), was originally posted to HMS AGGRESSIVE at Newhaven Harbour. He and RN Telegraphist Cyril Taylor were sent to find a couple of MTBs — there was some 'special operation' on that day needing extra operators. Fortunately for me, he writes, 'my boat had already left harbour — SO I'M STILL HERE!'

*Picture of Duchess of Kent visit. 18 March 1944. Commander Lilley (Front row, left); 3/O Bentley, 3/O Lyons (Middle row);Commander Stevens (Front row); Captain Heaton (Left of HRH); Supt WRNS (P) HRH Duchess of Kent; NOIC Captain Hardman-Jones (Right of HRH, hands clasped); Chief Officer Snow (Front row); 1/O Rowley (Front row); 2/O May (Middle row); 3/O Wickens (Front row); 3/O Phillips (Middle row); 3/O EJ De'Ath (Extreme right).*

(Newhaven Local & Maritime Museum, 1944)

*WRNS Yvonne Hastie Parker (now Groves), left, and two shipmates walk down Heighton Road circa November 1942. Behind them, the Nissen Hut Mess in the grounds of the Old Rectory.*

(Tom Bonnor, Three WRNS, 1942; © 1993)

*Heighton Road fifty years later. Only the distinctive roof features of the old Rectory are identifiable. Little wonder visiting veterans fail to recognise their former 'Wrennery'.*

(Tom Bonnor, 11 November 1993)

Vic met his future wife, WRNS Telegraphist Betty Smith, whilst serving at HMS FORWARD in 1944 and recalls their very first date. He took her to a cinema in Brighton and then to a restaurant. The service was slow and the meal was poor. Moreover, they missed both the last bus and the last train to Newhaven. They finally arrived (by Shanks's pony) at 0300hrs. Unfortunately Betty's shore leave expired at 2300hrs; so she was put 'in the rattle' the following day, and forfeited a day's leave and a day's pay!

Vic remembers that he and RN Telegraphist Reg Cannan were billeted with Mrs Crosthwaite, 'a delightful lady with two children' who lived in Putland Terrace in Denton. There was a large demand for temporary accommodation around Newhaven (and the entire south coast) during the war. Many families were able to supplement their meagre income by this means since the principal wage earner was usually at war on another front.

PRO documents record names of some local properties requisitioned by the War department in 1943 to supplement RN accommodation. These were No. 7, Southview; No. 2, Southdown Cottages; The Chapel; and Brighthaven, Denton Rise. It is known that Budehaven and Downside in Denton Rise accommodated HMS FORWARD WRNS annexed to the Old Rectory.

The Old Rectory in Heighton road was requisitioned as a 'Wrennery' about the time the Guinness Trust Holiday Home was requisitioned by the Admiralty although no details have been archived. There was a Nissen Hut in the garden (today, the driveway of St Clère) which was the Galley. Not everybody waxed eloquently of the quality of the food which was dispensed. WRNS Plotter Trixie Williams (now Gell) in particular wrote "When we came off duty at 8pm there would be an enamel jug of thick sludge called cocoa on the range. The spoon would be stood up straight in it!"

Many HMS FORWARD Wrens had to be billeted at Seaford in either Claremont House, Hughenden House, or Surrey House, an old gas-lit Victorian Convalescent Home with ancient bathrooms, now demolished, in Surrey Road. For a short while members of the WAAF were living in Surrey House. They were most annoyed about the strict régime suffered by the WRNS, that they had to be in quarters by 2230hrs in Summer and 2200hrs in Winter with one late pass a week to 2300hrs.

## A Disclaimer!

There is a belief that the tunnel is linked to Newhaven Fort; this incorrect assumption appears to originate from a statement made concerning a Royal Engineers Tunnelling Company which carried out excavations at both sites. A subterranean link would have served no purpose, and the cost would have been astronomical! Nor is there any truth in rumours that secret passages from here come up 'all over Denton.'

## Cuckmere Haven

Just south-west of the A259 bridge over the River Cuckmere at Exceat, is a small building which once contained electrical switching equipment and a direct telephone link back to HMS FORWARD telephone switchboard. Instructions to operate the switching equipment were issued directly from HMS FORWARD to troops guarding Exceat bridge.

In Newhaven Square a time capsule is located in the footway which bears the following text . . .

*"To save Newhaven from German bombing in the 1939/45 war, a replica of the harbour lighting system was set up at Cuckmere Haven. When a raid began the electricity was cut OFF at Newhaven and turned ON over Cuckmere marshes often successfully diverting enemy planes. Consequently only 409 bombs hit the town killing few people."*

It cannot have been a pleasant duty to have to entice the enemy to drop his bombs on yourself!

Documents held by the PRO suggest that another tactic of the decoy lighting was to entice enemy navigators to make erroneous calculations thereby deflecting them from their intended target. Little attention was accorded the fact that enemy navigation was for the most part guided by radio beams rather than the pilot looking out of the window!

# HMS FORWARD — A SYNOPSIS

Why was it necessary to have a Naval Headquarters at Newhaven? The answer is fairly complex, and evolved in response to the changing misfortunes of our immediate European neighbours. To appreciate fully the evolutionary aspects, it is necessary to consider the increasingly menacing situation resulting from the rapid advancement of the theatre of war. Germany invaded Denmark, Norway, Holland, Belgium, Luxembourg and France in 1940. Following the fall of France, England faced the threat of invasion. A glance at key dates in the early history of the war illustrates the cause for concern . . .

03-09-39  Britain and France declared war on Germany.
11-09-39  British troops on French soil.
09-04-40  Germany invaded Denmark and Norway.
10-05-40  Germany invaded Holland, Belgium and Luxembourg.
27-05-40  Dunkirk evacuation.
05-06-40  Hitler proclaimed war of total annihilation against enemies.
08-06-40  German armoured forces penetrated French defences near Rouen.
10-06-40  Italy declared war on Britain and France.
22-06-40  France accepted terms for Armistice.
01-07-40  Channel Islands invaded.
10-07-40  Battle of Britain began.

Geographically, Newhaven lies roughly midway between Dover and Portsmouth and has the only other river navigable at all states of the tide. Economically, Newhaven was equipped with Marine workshops and facilities for maintaining cross-channel steamers and vessels with up to 19ft tail shaft. The port had ample berthing and a marine passenger terminal with a dedicated railway terminus. All this made Newhaven a desirable prize to the enemy.

With the fall of France, Newhaven was on the front line, and no time was lost in building up the Naval base. The Admiralty requisitioned the Guinness Trust Holiday Home and set up a Headquarters there from 20 June, to 31 August, 1945. An Admiralty directive of March, 1941, called for Naval Plots to be established at specified locations. Excavation of a tunnel commenced in July, 1941, which was used from late 1941 until abandoned on 21 November, 1945. During that period, the following dates were significant . . .

11-02-42  Scharnhorst, Gneiseneau & Prinz Eugen sail up Channel.
19-08-42  Dieppe raid.
04-06-44  D-Day.
13-06-44  First V1 fell on England at Swanscombe.
10-07-44  Rouen liberated.
25-08-44  Paris liberated.
03-09-44  Allies in Belgium.
08-09-44  First V2 fell on England.
08-05-45  End of WWII against Germany officially declared.
15-08-45  VJ Day.
31-08-45  Admiralty decommissioned HMS FORWARD .
21-11-45  East entrance to tunnel sealed.

The following extracts are from PRO file ADM1/18136 "HMS FORWARD, Newhaven Sub-Command 1939–45, History of War Activities."

On 25 August, 1939, initial preparations for the maritime militarisation of Newhaven were put in place. Newhaven was commissioned as a commercial point, the officers taking up appointments on instructions from the Admiralty. A number of Ratings (about forty), mostly pensioners, also joined and were accommodated in the RNVR Drill Hall in Bridge Street which made an excellent Naval Barracks for a small number.

The initial staff of the Naval Officer-in-Charge was Captain AA Lovett-Cameron (Naval Officer-in-Charge), Paymaster Commander LS Brown (Base Accountant Officer), one Paymaster Lieut-Commander, and three Paymaster Sub-Lieuts so it will be seen that Paymasters had to do the duty of Duty Officers in addition to their own ordinary duties (This was not arduous at this early date because few Naval Bases had much in the way of telephone or teleprinter communications and visitors were not arriving at all hours). In addition to the Naval Officer-in-Charge there was a Sea Transport Officer and his staff, an Army Movements Control Officer and his staff, a Col. RAMC (ADMS) and his staff, and an Army Security Officer (MI5) and his staff.

On Admiralty instructions the Base became self-contained with its own ledgers and was commissioned as "HMS FORWARD ", a small tug, the Seaton, being requisitioned as name ship. The Base developed rapidly and smoothly including the Port War Signal Station under the Admiral Commanding Reserves. The ordinary cross channel services, both passenger and goods, continued. One large steam train being run down each evening for this purpose and leaving for London again the following morning. The examination service was also brought into being, and the Southern Railway Harbour Master was commissioned as the Commander RNR. Difficulty was experienced chartering suitable vessels but these were eventually found.

In November, 1939, the first four WRNS were entered and being local inhabitants were immobile. In January, 1940, an Executive Officer was appointed for the first time thus giving relief to the Accountant Officers, and another WRNS was appointed.

Newhaven was originally scheduled to be the casualty clearing station for casualties from France, and there was some discussion whether it could not be demilitarised and declared an 'open town' under the Geneva Red Cross Convention. It carried sick hospital carriers with twelve fully equipped hospital trains and these were used for the conveyance of wounded and sick from the continent and for the conveyance of medical supplies to the Army in France. In addition, the loading and dispatch of coasters with every conceivable item of supplies for the Army were organised at Newhaven and Littlehampton.

Towards the end of May, 1940, it was decided to start a Naval Officer Mess independently of the London & Paris Hotel (later named "HMS AGGRESSIVE") and the Sheffield Hotel on the west side was requisitioned. This was to accommodate twelve officers and the Base ship's office. A further increase of WRNS took place when the Sheffield Hotel was commissioned. The WRNS then on duty were telephone operators, SDO (Signals Distribution Office) messengers, Stewards and Cooks, and most of them were mobile. A Third Officer WRNS (Administrative) was appointed. The expansion of the WRNS subsequently took its usual course until they eventually reached the figure of five hundred with a large number of WRNS Officers.

Air raids, of course, with nights in shelters were a frequent occurrence.

The Dunkirk epic. At the end of May, 1940, craft started to pour into Newhaven from the west with a view to their being kitted up and sent to Dover for Operation DYNAMO. These craft of all sizes literally came in hundreds and it will be realised that material was not on the spot to meet all requirements. Admiralty and Dockyard departments could not have been more helpful and the London Dems supplied such rifles and Lewis guns as they could spare. One problem was fresh water but this was eventually solved by borrowing from the Army five gallon water containers. All craft were thus sent on in time with food, water, armament and medical supplies including hypodermic syringes with morphia.

Operation DYNAMO was followed by Operation CYCLE which was organised from Portsmouth with assistance from Newhaven. For Operation CYCLE a large number of professional fishermen were entered up on T124 which worked out very well. A Belgian canal tug in excellent condition landed refugees at Hastings and was brought to Newhaven by the Lifeboat's crew. This craft was commissioned on a civilian basis with the tug's crew, named CARDY and kept in use at Newhaven until the end of 1944.

Dunkirk completely altered the organisation of Newhaven. Sea transport, movements, control and medical services were withdrawn and it meant that the port had to be put on a defensive basis. The Army quite rightly wanted the Sheffield Hotel as a strong point, and therefore a Naval Officers Mess was formed in the Guinness Trust Holiday Home, Denton, a very suitable building which was developed as Naval Headquarters with offices and living accommodation under one roof.

The staff now started to increase very rapidly and requisitioning of suitable premises took place to meet the demands for housing of Ratings, WRNS, etc.

One point which should not be overlooked was the organisation of the Auxiliary Patrol immediately after Dunkirk. Various craft were used in forming five sections with six boats each with a subsidiary section at Littlehampton. A Headquarters was formed in the Missions to Seamen hut on west side, which also provided for messing and recreation. The craft were not very suitable for the work in the winter months, but the inshore patrol was maintained.

In 1941 Coastal Force Base was started with one ML flotilla and it was anticipated that it would increase to seven flotillas. This meant further expansion on the East quay with the requisitioning of buildings from the Southern Railway for issue rooms, Naval stores, etc. Also during 1941, a controlled minefield was laid outside of the harbour entrance with an operation room in the Fort alongside the Port War Signals Station. Small minefields were also laid at Shoreham and Littlehampton.

An Admiralty direction of March, 1941, ordered certain named ports to establish and maintain Naval plots. A coastal chain for radar surface watching was started in the Dover area. It soon spread to cover Newhaven and this necessitated a Naval Plot at Newhaven. In order to accommodate this plot with adequate security and all the necessary communications equipment at the new Headquarters site, it was decided to burrow deep into Heighton Hill.

A boom was required at Newhaven and Shoreham and pending any other suitable arrangements vessels were sunk to narrow the channel and a block ship was in place which could be pulled across the opening by wires and sunk in position as required. All the necessary equipment for a fire boom was also installed. Naval six inch guns were mounted in pairs at suitable intervals along the coast manned by Naval Ratings to start with, the Army taking them over later. Anti-aircraft protection was given by BOFERS guns of Royal Artillery situated at the Fort and suitable sites around the harbour.

A fire boom was installed early in 1942 to operate across the narrows arranged so as to swing across from west to east. The oil and pump house was stowed in the Fort Moat. Later that year, the derricks and boom were carried away by an LCT when entering the harbour, and it was then abolished. Mine watching posts were built into the west quayside and manned by Southern Railway workers.

This period to the next epic was filled with the Battle of Britain etc, and various parties for "snoops" on the French coast were organised and started from Newhaven or Shoreham.

Admiral Hardman-Jones (serving in the rank of Captain) relieved Captain Lovett-Cameron as Naval Officer-in-Charge in 1942.

On 19 August, 1942, was the Dieppe raid, but before this took place, the abortive effort to exchange prisoners of war with Germany failed. The German prisoners actually remained in Newhaven for three days, and night after night at about 0130hrs the vessels shortened in, lights were put on as agreed, and then orders came through for a mark-time.

The Dieppe raid was the largest undertaking that Newhaven had had for some time, and a very considerable amount of organisation was required. On the actual day, in the afternoon, 750 men were fed at the 'Hide' up the river in a field under the trees and eventually the Queens Own Cameron Highlanders (who had been at one time, the holding Batallion at Newhaven) were embarked in small landing craft and sailed after dusk for Dieppe. It had been stated that no returning parties would come to Newhaven, but it was just as well that provision was made against this idea, because on one evening over 2000 extra meals were served and nearly a thousand were bedded down for the night.

One valuable contribution to the Dieppe raid is that their Naval Plot had to organise and run the Air/Sea Rescue work for the expedition, and did it very creditably. Many crashed aircraft crews were picked up.

After Dieppe, life went on without much excitement. Craft increased in Coastal Forces, and of different types, being used for patrols and raids. CE and CW convoys proceeded on their way with the occasional raids by German E-boats. Radar developed and decoys were discussed and established. Three MFVs were kept from the disbanded Auxiliary Patrol and when the service allowed were used for fishing to amplify the local diet.

During the latter part of 1943, intimations began to be received that the organisation for D-Day should be built up. Landing craft had begun to appear at Newhaven and Shoreham, and "HMS LIZARD" at Hove and "HMS NEWT" at Newhaven had been commissioned. Exercises with Landing craft were carried out and the lessons learned in the Sicily landing were studied.

The Vice-Admiral RV Halt was appointed as Naval Officer-in-Charge in early 1944, and was succeeded by Vice-Admiral Sir TJ Hallett in October, 1944.

A full report on the three phases of D-Day has been rendered ie the "build up", D-Day, and the "aftermath", and details need not be given here. Sufficient is it to mention that requisitions went on and personnel gradually increased until there were over ten thousand on HMS FORWARD 's ledgers. Special arrangements were made to make sub-commands self-supporting and this meant covering HMS MARLBOROUGH at Eastbourne, Newhaven and HMS NEWT, HMS LIZARD at Hove, Resident Naval Officer Shoreham, and Resident Naval Officer Littlehampton. A large victualling depot was established at Lewes, and Burgess Hill was available for Naval stores which had been increased considerably to cover permanent, consumable, and after action stores. Naval canteen service was made complete for the area. Special oil tanks were built and developed under the Base Engineer Officer, and emergency repair overseers were appointed under a Principal Emergency Repair Overseer. Special Sick Quarters were requisitioned and fully staffed and equipped. As already mentioned, numerous large establishments had been requisitioned at Seaford for the accommodation of the WRNS. Seaford was chosen as it was the nearest town which could provide the requisite houses.

It was decided to reduce the Newhaven Sub-Command to the status of Resident Naval Officer on 7 July, 1945. This appointment was abolished on 15 August, 1945, during which time arrangements were made for de-requisitioning all properties and dismantling of the local defences. The status of Newhaven area as a full sub-command was never definitely established by Admiralty order mainly because various C-in-C's at Portsmouth did not seem to want it so. It is a fact that it was always treated almost as such except that the NOIC did not correspond direct with the Admiralty but always referred to the C-in-C Portsmouth.

## Author's notes

HMS FORWARD was a shore based ship which knew several venues in Newhaven during the early months of the war. The original venue was the RNVR Hall (now demolished) in Bridge Street, at which time East Side and the London & Paris Hotel became known as HMS FORWARD II according to the Paybooks of one veteran and his wife.

Nominal Depot Ships for HMS FORWARD were S.S. "Sefton" from 13 September, 1939, to 20 June, 1941; Motor Boat "Spitfire" from 20 June, 1941, to 11 November, 1941; and "White Orchid" from 11 November, 1941, to 7 July, 1945.

This information is corroborated by Lt. Commander Ivor Howcroft (Rtd) who adds that the Sussex Division RNVR closed on 12 October, 1939, when the Drill Hall was taken into use as the Base. HMS FORWARD II existed from 4 March, 1941, to 4 November, 1942, with "White Spray" as the Nominal Depot Ship for that period. From this period onwards, HMS FORWARD II was renamed HMS AGGRESSIVE.

For a brief period in May, 1940, the Sheffield Hotel became an Officers Mess for HMS FORWARD. The Westminster Bank at Newhaven was used by HMS FORWARD Paymaster Captain. It appears there were some seventy-eight Paywriters and Stores personnel serving here according to a 1944 photograph.

WRNS Certificates of Service for 1944 show both HMS FORWARD and HMS FORWARD II for Wrens working both in the tunnel and as Boats Crew at the port. The continued use of this suffix defies reason; certainly no other known official documentation relates to HMS FORWARD II.

The Special Sick Quarters referred to in PRO notes above is Gracie Fields former home in Dorothy Avenue, Peacehaven. Extended in 1972, it is now a residential home called "Dorothy House".

## A Complementary Complimentary Signal

The following signal was received at HMS FORWARD by teleprinter at 1600hrs 4 September, 1944. The signal was retyped with an Imperial machine, and duplicated with a Meths machine believed to be an Ormig. The signal had been copied onto the reverse side of a Naval Message form S1320e.

TO: PORTSMOUTH COMMAND. FROM: C IN C. PORTSMOUTH.
(R) ADMIRALTY. ANCXF. COMMANDER IN CHIEF PLYMOUTH.
A.C.DOVER. A O C IN C C. C. G O C IN C SOUTHERN COMMAND.

THE FIRST BATTLE OF THE CHANNEL WAS WAGED AND WON IN 1940–1942 WITH THE DEFEAT OF THE ATTEMPT BY THE GERMAN AIR FORCE TO DESTROY OUR COASTAL CONVOYS AND CAUSE SERIOUS EMBARRASSMENT FOR OUR WAR INDUSTRIES AND ECONOMIC LIFE.

2. WHAT MAY WELL BE DESCRIBED AS THE SECOND BATTLE OF THE CHANNEL IS DRAWING TO A DRAMATIC CLOSE WITH THE ECLIPSE OF THE GERMAN NAVAL FORCES IN THIS AREA, DUE TO A COMBINATION OF NAVAL, MILITARY AND AIR ACTION.

3. THE SECOND BATTLE OF THE CHANNEL MAY BE DIVIDED INTO THREE PERIODS:
(A) THE DEFENCE OF OUR COASTAL CONVOYS DURING 1942–1944 FROM E-BOAT ATTACK.
(B) THE PREPARATION FOR THE INVASION OF EUROPE AND THE LAUNCHING FROM THIS COMMAND OF THE MAJOR PORTION OF THE ASSAULT FORCES.
(C) THE SUPPLY OF THE ALLIED ARMIES IN FRANCE AND THE PROTECTION OF THE CROSS CHANNEL ROUTE FROM U-BOAT AND E-BOAT ATTACK.

4. THE PORTSMOUTH NAVAL COMMAND HAS PLAYED AN ESSENTIAL PART IN THIS BATTLE AND ITS SUCCESSFUL CONCLUSION IS DUE TO THE UNTIRING DEVOTION TO DUTY OF ALL THE OFFICERS AND RATINGS CONCERNED, BOTH BY SEA AND SHORE.

5. BEFORE THE DISPERSAL ELSEWHERE OF THE STRONG FORCES LENT TEMPORARILY TO THE COMMAND DURING POSSIBLY THE MOST VITAL PERIOD IN ITS HISTORY, I WISH TO EXPRESS MY UNBOUNDED ADMIRATION OF THE ENERGY, SKILL AND ENDURANCE DISPLAYED BY THE FLAG OFFICERS,COMMODORES, COMMANDING OFFICERS, OFFICERS AND SHIPS' COMPANIES OF ALL H M SHIPS AND ESTABLISHMENTS CONCERNED, COASTAL FORCES AND LANDING CRAFT AND MEMBERS OF THE W R N S, WHOM I HAVE HAD THE HONOUR TO COMMAND OR DIRECT.

6. ESPECIAL PRAISE IS DUE TO MAGNIFICENT WORK OF THE ENGINE ROOM DEPARTMENTS AND THE REPAIR ORGANISATIONS BY WHICH SO MANY SHIPS HAVE BEEN ABLE TO ANSWER THE CONTINUAL CALLS MADE UPON THEM.

7. THE BRAVERY INVARIABLY SHOWN BY ALL THOSE IN CONTACT WITH THE ENEMY AS EXEMPLIFIED BY THE RECENT FRUITFUL NIGHT ACTIONS OFF CAP D'ANTIFER HAS CROWNED ANY SUCCESS WE HAVE ACHIEVED AS A WHOLE AND IS IN KEEPING WITH THE HIGHEST TRADITIONS OF OUR GREAT SERVICE.

8. I ASK ALL HANDS TO ACCEPT MY SINCERE GRATITUDE, THANKS AND CONGRATULATIONS. (041600.B.SEPT).

DIST:NOIC.SOO.DSO.PSO.SEC.CDR.BAO.PAY(S).EOS.COREP. SQ.CDR. LT.CDR.M/S. ADO. AGG. NEWT. SHOREHAM. LIZARD. L'HAMPTON. NAVAL BASE. 1/O.WRNS. CO.WRNS. PSTO.PWSS. BEACHY. NCSO. DEMS.ERO.LOG. DOCG. ST.BEDES. MARLBORO' D.SIG.O. SDO.

SYSTEM: T/P. TOR,041905.

# TUNNEL DESIGN, EXCAVATION & CONSTRUCTION

In 1941 Col. FH Foster DSO OBE TD DL RIBA CRE 4 Corps Troops Engineers, (previously Commanding Officer of 210 (Sussex) Field Company Royal Engineers) designed a new underground HQ at Newhaven for the Naval Officer in Charge (NOIC) and staff, with a big signal operations room, and Headquarters for both the Canadian Corps Coastal Artillery serving the area, and the Home Guard. In a telephone conversation of July, 1993, Col Foster (then approaching his ninetieth birthday) revealed that he designed the Heighton Hill establishment after visiting Montgomery's subterranean headquarters in the North Downs near Reigate. Excavation commenced in July, 1941, and fitting out was completed by December.

The underground establishment was designed to accommodate all the vital communications eg W/T, plotting, coding, telephone exchange, SDO, and cabins and mess rooms for personnel on day and night watches. The tunnel was ventilated by air-conditioning machinery fitted with gas filters at 65°. Special daylight lighting was installed in the offices. Four machine gun posts guarded the approaches, and an observation post with full view of the harbour and surrounding hills was installed, disguised as a chicken house.

Information regarding the excavation of the tunnel has been provided by Mr William Wild, an Officer with 172 Tunnelling Company. "From July, 1941, to July, 1942, the 1st Tunnelling Engineers Group was stationed at Tunbridge Wells under CRE Lt-Col. Hill RE, MC. At that time there were three Companies, 170 based in Gibraltar, 171 based in Dover, and 172 based in Tunbridge Wells, with its four sections split up.

"No.1 Section built an underground HQ at Tunbridge Wells. No.2 Section served at Newhaven and South Heighton under the command of Major Lindsay Fox (a Canadian, who at the outbreak of the war had been working in London as a Mining Engineer with Union Corporation Ltd). No.3 Section served at Tunbridge Wells and later in south Sussex building underground resistance facilities, and No.4 Section spent all its time building the latter. After completing the work in the Newhaven area, No.2 Section built a small hospital at Folkestone. They went on to Canterbury, Dover, Portsmouth and Plymouth before being sent to Gibraltar."

The Canadian Army had a small drilling section which was employed at South Heighton drilling the vertical shafts from the surface to the tunnels below for antenna cables, forced ventilation and the stand-by generator exhaust.

Royal Engineers No.577 Army Field Company was engaged in the construction under Major R Hawker who had been an engineer with Brighton Corporation until the outbreak of war. Harry R Francis, an RE 577 Coy driver, who had conveyed construction materials to the site, responded to my appeal for information. Sadly, Harry suffered a fatal heart attack before we could exchange further correspondence.

## Construction

The tunnel labyrinth comprises some 350 linear yards (320m) of minor galleries and 227 linear yards (208m) of major galleries from which a calculated 3475 cubic yards (2650 cubic metres) of chalk (6070 tons) were excavated using pneumatic hand drills known as 'punchers'. These quantities were probably well exceeded since it is impossible to drill a perfectly dimensioned tunnel through chalk owing to the nature of the material.

Small dumper trucks with less than full loads transported most of the chalk to the former South Heighton Cement Works Quarry where freshly quarried chalk would be quite natural and some was used at Sleepers Hole on West Side to create a tank loading ramp for embarkation purposes.

Some of the spoil was used to build the embankment approaches to a military Hamilton Bridge across the River Ouse at Southease strong enough to carry 40-ton tanks. Upon completion, Col. Foster invited the Commander of a Churchill tank squadron to test out the bridge, and the next day they went together to see a convoy of twenty tanks (each weighing 40 tons) make a successful crossing.

Shortly afterwards Col. Foster received an irate phone call from an Ouse River Board official complaining that a tank had broken the timber ribbons of their three ton limit swing bridge. It later transpired that they had seen only nineteen tanks cross the new bridge. One tank had broken down some miles back, and had left the column. The crew completed their repairs and carried on, but in spite of new direction boards, they crossed the three ton limit swing bridge instead of the Hamilton!

The tunnel is reinforced with standard mining ironwork sections which consist of interleaved galvanised corrugated iron sheets supported by pairs of curved rolled steel joists which have been fishplated together at roof level and braced at floor level to maintain separation. The fishplates are embossed "GKS CARDIFF British Steel" — products of Guest & Keen Steelworks of Cardiff. Adjacent pairs of RSJs are linked horizontally with six prefabricated nitched iron bars, which interlock with preformed slots in the RSJs to maintain a standard separation, secured with wedges.

Horizontal bends in the tunnel are created by using a number of special angled sections as required. Right-angled corners, end stops, and vertical bends (for tops and bottoms of stairs), were produced in 'kit' form. Stairwells were constructed from standard components tilted 30 degrees from horizontal. This method of construction facilitated and hastened the completion of the work.

## Lingering Impressions

Entering the tunnel one is obsessed by countless thoughts pertaining to the construction and use of the tunnel. Some conceptions have been inspired by piecing together known facts and logically considering the evidence. Let us return to the summer of 1941, to the excavation and lining of the galleries by the Royal Engineers.

*Excavation of West entrance Summer 1941. Unique photograph showing camouflaged workings and vehicle 'hide' in the foreground.*

(Tom Bonnor; © 1993)

In July a camouflaged canopy was constructed over a natural cleft in the roadside bank destined to become the western entrance. Photographs record the early appearance of this construction as tunnelling began. The pick marks of the sappers, who used pneumatic hand picks (punchers), are preserved for posterity in some exposed gallery walls. The excavated spoil was extracted via the western entrance using a narrow gauge miners tramway. This tramway also transported copious quantities of heavy preformed rolled steel joists and corrugated galvanised steel lining back to the chalk face as work progressed. These facts are supported in archived photographs and a discarded puncher found on site.

Chalk spoil was loaded into the trams by hand, pushed manually to the west entrance, and discharged down a chute into waiting dumper trucks. The trams then returned to the face for the next load. As excavation progressed it was necessary to extend the tunnel lining and the tramway track, increasing the distance to transport spoil and materials to and from the entrance. Calculations indicate that some 6500 'return journeys' were made by these trams, clocking up an incredible 1080 miles (1728km) in total.

*Sentry on guard at the entrance to the workings. Chalk spoil being discharged into chute at railhead. Note whistle hanging on left side of portal, used for air raid and gas attack warnings.*
(© IWM; Photo 14501, 2 October 1941)

Work was hard enough on the level parts of the excavations, but even harder on the inclined sections where the thirty degree slopes (for stairways) not only made tunnelling difficult, but also prevented immediate access to the trams. Whilst the spoil would slide to the bottom of the inclines, there were some elevated level galleries (landings) where the spoil required multiple manual handling. The number of miners and labourers increased considerably after the first one hundred yards of narrow access gallery was completed. From this point onwards, work was carried out on several advancing faces simultaneously, and the extraction and disposal of the increased volume of chalk spoil became the limiting factor.

The problem of the chalk disposal did not end at the tunnel mouth. The enemy had already occupied northern France; Sussex was on the front line and enemy reconnaissance aircraft were expected at any time. The possibility of photographic disclosure of the existence of the tunnel had to be avoided. No hint of chalk on the road could be tolerated. A Lysander aircraft overflew the area occasionally checking for give-away tracks on the tarmac.

South Heighton Farmer Ab Eldridge remembers that initially some chalk was used to make a raised causeway into the meadows across the road opposite Hampden Gardens only a couple of hundred yards away. This practice was promptly abandoned when it was reported that the virgin white chalk drew attention to the area, and the deposited spoil was quickly covered with top soil and turf.

Meanwhile, above the tunnel four hillside pillboxes were being constructed beneath a great swathe of camouflage. I watched the foundations and walls of these pillboxes being cast with masses of concrete, reinforcing, and corrugated iron shuttering, too young to appreciate their purpose.

Back underground, close on the heels of the miners, followed the RE fitters who first of all manhandled the three large 450 gallon (2040l) water tanks to their current locations. These tanks are incarcerated for eternity; they will never pass through the restricted passageways subsequently constructed.

During fitting out there was a great demand for temporary lighting, flagstones, timber noggins and battens, roofing felt, plywood, engineering bricks, breeze-blocks, shuttering, reinforcement, sand, cement, aggregate, and water.

The floors and footways in the main and access galleries were paved with 1400 flagstones; considerable quantities of waterproof bitumen felt and plywood were used to line an estimated 20,000 square feet of tunnel sides and partitions.

All the evidence points to the lining of the larger galleries with roofing felt and plywood as an early stage of customising the interior. Before the actual lining could be applied it was necessary to wedge noggins of 4ins x 2ins (100 x 50mm) timber between the channelling of adjacent RSJs which would eventually serve to support everything which needed to be suspended (lighting, cable-tray, ventilation trunking) or fixed to the sides (shelves, notice boards, benches, etc). This demanded a lot of forethought and much timber.

Next came the preparations for attaching the plywood lining. Fourteen parallel 2·5ins x 1ins (62 x 25mm) wooden battens were secured horizontally to the RSJs at 18ins (457mm) spacing the whole length of the large galleries. Each batten was secured to each RSJ with a twist of galvanised wire at every intersection. In total, there is more than 660ft of large gallery with RSJs every 34ins (860mm), so there are approximately 234 RSJs. A swift calculation shows that some 9240ft (2·8Km) of batten was used, secured to the RSJs with more than 3250 twists of wire! The plywood was later tacked to the battening with the roofing felt sandwiched between to provide a waterproof membrane. Finally, many gallons of whitewash were used to brighten the offices.

After the lining had been fixed, air ducting, permanent lighting, and cable-trays for carrying the power and communications cables were installed.

By a rare stroke of fortune, one Lieut Tanner visited the site on 2 October, 1941, to take photographs of "an underground operation control centre under construction somewhere in SE Command." Eight photographs in the Imperial War Museum archives, can be positively identified as belonging to this site. Taken at various locations, they provide a unique insight into the priorities and the progress at that date, and four have been included in this book. They show excavation was complete except for the pillbox access galleries. The long east exit stairways were almost finished, and one area of the operational centre was hastily fitted out for a posed picture to suggest it was already in operation; but in truth, at this moment much basic installation still remained to be done.

The stand-by engine, generator and other large plant items were clearly installed before the west air-lock was built because it was necessary to remove the air-lock armour plate door and its frame, and demolish some associated brickwork in order to retrieve the equipment after the war.

Several thousand hard engineering bricks embossed "Warnham S B Co" were used in the construction of the Denton House exit, the grenade pit, the machine gun posts, the bottom of the chicken house shaft, the firing screen, the east air-lock, the underfloor air ducts, the western air-lock, and the western exit. More than 2000 breeze-blocks were used to build partitions and walls. Considerable quantities of concrete were used to bed-in every RSJ, build plinths for the air-conditioning equipment, stand-by engine, and other items of plant, and form 178 steps. Externally, many tons of concrete were used in the construction of the four hillside pillboxes, the mock chicken house, the roof of the west exit, and the western end steps down to road level.

Considerable electrical installation work was required for the air-conditioning equipment, stand-by generator, normal and emergency lighting, and power sockets for the radio receivers, transmitters, teleprinters, battery chargers (for telephone exchange batteries, and emergency lighting batteries) and also for heating equipment in the galley for hot drinks. External telephone cables entered the establishment by both entrances. Telephones and teleprinters had to be installed. Aerial feeder cables had to be provided. Flights of wooden stairs to the pillboxes had to be made in situ. The list is neither comprehensive nor complete.

*"Sappers" finishing off one of the long stairways leading to an exit. Identified as flight of fifty-one stairs to Guinness Trust exit. Note bucket suspended on a rope to avoid contact with fresh screed surfaces.*

(© IWM; Photo H 14508, 2 October 1941)

*Stairs to east end exit. This is the view from the machine gun post with the 1943 gate halfway up the stairs. Compare this with IWM H14508 (above) which is the same view.*

(Tom Bonnor, 1993)

Let us consider what is known about the electrical distribution in the tunnel. Three phase electrical power was normally obtained from the public electricity supplies via an underground cable which terminated in a distribution case in a small room off the stairway to the Guinness Trust Holiday Home. Evidence indicates that a cable led from this room via floor trunking to some cable-tray, and by a route no longer discernible, eventually arrived at the switching and distribution frame in the air-conditioning room. Floor channelling indicates how cables from the stand-by generator also reached this frame which contained the switchgear to select the preferred power source.

Official records in the Public Records Office at Kew state that "Special daylight lighting was installed in the offices." Today we are familiar with fluorescent light, but in 1941 it was very new having been invented only in 1938. The principle virtues of this form of lighting are its efficiency (more light for less watts) and shadowless lighting. A wartime photograph taken in a another operational establishment shows eight fluorescent lamps (presumably 4ft 40W) being used to illuminate a 30ft (9m) gallery. Illuminating HMS FORWARD operational centre to a similar standard would have required 5kW of electrical power. Lighting the long access galleries by normal incandescent lamps to a reduced standard would have required at least another 1·5kW.

The official records also reveal a temperature of 65° was maintained in the tunnel. This was achieved by passing the air through a multi-kilowatt heater and explains the reason for the reinforced concrete pillars in the air-conditioning room; they supported the heating unit which would have been extremely hot.

Forced air ventilation passed from the air-conditioning room to the two main galleries via a large cement lined underfloor duct which had spurs to the galley and the most westerly interconnecting tunnel. At each of the four locations where the air emerged from below floor a regulator was fitted into the trunking. Further regulation was possible at each louvre. To improve airflow within the centre, all walls and partitions had perforated zinc hatches.

To further encourage air circulation, additional high-level trunking was installed to collect stale air and expel it. Evidence of an electric fan for this purpose exists in the eastern air-lock where air was discharged through trunking running up the stairs. Similarly, another large shaft rises vertically from the SDO in the southernmost inter-connecting tunnel.

## Toilets and foul water

Four Elsan chemical toilets were installed underground; two of these were located outside the operations centre air-lock at the west end, and had a makeshift metal trough supported by a rough wooden frame as a wash basin. Two others were located inside the west air-lock near the galley. Under conditions of siege or attack when the armour plate doors were sealed, only these two Elsan toilets would have been available to the concealed workforce! The severely rusted remains of one Elsan toilet unit was found in the fan room when some toppled air trunking was moved. The enamelled bucket insert associated with this toilet was also discovered, in excellent condition and brimful of crystal clear water.

*Engineers at work on excavations for a ventilation duct. Identified as northmost interconnecting gallery (see also page 34). A pile of breeze-blocks is just visible in the distance.*

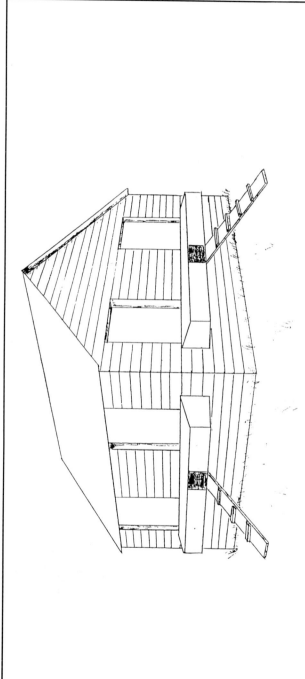

EXTERNAL APPEARANCE OF THE MOCK HEN HOUSE PILLBOX 1941 - 1945.
HEIGHTON HILL, NEWHAVEN. NAVAL OPERATIONS INTELLIGENCE CENTRE.
LOCATED NGR TQ 4503 0269

Defending the West end of the Guinness Trust Holiday Home and the
Antenna installations, it was accessed internally by a wooden ladder
in a 20ft vertical shaft reached by 83 stairs (in 3 flights) from the
Operations Centre.

© G. ELLIS.
18 . FEB 1993.

*External appearance of the Observation Post 1941–45 (see also page 63).*
(Geoffrey Ellis, 18 February 1993)

There was no provision for waste water drainage from either the sinks in the galley or the toilet; what appear to be drains are in fact two adjacent cavities about 18ins square and 24ins deep (457 x 457 x 610mm) which are connected about 12ins (300mm) below floor level. One of these cavities contained a water strainer — a hardwood frame 17ins square x 9.5ins deep (432 x 432 x 240mm) with a perforated zinc bottom. Used water was discharged into the filter and allowed to flow into the second chamber which had a capacity of 25 gallons (110l). It is therefore not unreasonable to conclude that it was somebody's duty to carefully monitor the contents of waste water sumps and the Elsan toilets and discharge the effluent via the external toilet block at the west exit.

## Pillboxes and Emergency exit

The communications centre was defended by five pillboxes accessible from within, and one externally accessible pillbox at the western entrance. By far the most remarkable of these was the mock hen house observation post which stood alone at the east end of the complex at NGR TQ45030269.

This observation post was constructed of reinforced concrete, but the external shuttering was a chicken shed which remained a permanent feature. The window frames contained mock wooden louvres, and the four side gun ports were convincingly disguised with instantly detachable outboard nesting boxes and chicken ramps. It stood in a wire mesh enclosure complete with Rhode Island Reds whose access was strictly limited only to the nesting boxes.

The hen house observation post stood just 60yds (55m) from the west wing of the Guinness Trust Holiday Home in an open field giving cover to the antenna masts as well as the entrance and

*The observation post which commanded extensive views and provided an emergency exit from the tunnel. Access was via a vertical shaft from below. Convincingly disguised as a wooden chicken shed its gun ports were covered by detachable outboard nesting boxes. Live chicken completed the illusion. By 1964, it had lost its timber jacket and awaited demolition. During the war the nearest buildings were Southview Terrace and the Guinness Trust Holiday Home. The houses now seen (rear of Brands Close) are more recent. This pillbox stood on ground which is now the rear garden of 28 Glynde Close (see also page 62).*

(Geoffrey Ellis, June 1964; © 1996)

west end of the Holiday Home. It was accessed internally by an unprepared wooden ladder in a 20ft (6m) vertical timber lined shaft reached by fifty-six stairs (in two flights) from the grenade pit landing. Braby cable-tray attached to the walls of the access stairway suggests that aerial feeder coaxial cables and internal telephone communications cables were also routed this way to the surface.

An emergency escape hatch was cast into the east wall at low level. This consisted of a strong metal frame, just large enough for a person to wriggle through, set into the fabric of the pillbox, with a thick steel plate securely attached to the frame by a number of blind bolts accessible only from within. In the event of serious damage to the normal exits, this would have been used for evacuation.

Further down the hill were the four semi-submerged pillboxes at 40–100ft (12–30m) intervals. These pillboxes were about 12ft (4m) in overall diameter, cast in reinforced concrete with walls and roof about 2ft (0·6m) thick. Each pillbox had four corbelled gun loops with openings about 1ft square, each affording 90° arcs of fire. The pillboxes were covered with earth and turf and were virtually invisible from the air. They were only accessible from within the tunnel by climbing flights of wooden steps ascending from the west end air-lock to a point beneath the pillbox, and climbing a 9ft wooden ladder (made from unprepared timber) into the pillbox. The pillboxes were some 50ft (15m) above the level of the operations centre.

Materials to construct these pillboxes were conveyed from the top of the hill on a miner's narrow gauge tramway which was temporarily installed along a public footpath (now Brands Close) which then led from the South Heighton Post Office down to West View Terrace passing the southernmost pillbox. Here, the tramway turned northwards to the other pillbox sites under a swathe of camouflage.

Two of the four pillboxes were sited on ground now occupied by Nos. 15 & 19 Glynde Close with the engine cooling shaft in between them at No. 17 Glynde Close. This 50ft (15m) shaft was lined with galvanised-iron sleeving approximately 10·5ins (267mm) diameter, and also contained the 4ins (100mm) exhaust pipe for the emergency power generator). Heat from the engine radiator was expelled through this shaft with fan assistance. The other two pillboxes were sited in the rear gardens of Nos. 33 & 37 Heighton Close.

*A gun port of one of four hillside pillboxes. Soil erosion reveals detail of its construction.*

(Geoffrey Ellis, June 1964; © 1996)

*Looking through a hillside pillbox to the opposite gun loop. Each turret had four such loops with mountings for Vickers machine guns.*

(Geoffrey Ellis, June 1964; © 1996)

*Hillside pillbox access. A vertical wooden ladder dropped about nine feet to the access tunnel beneath. Note the iron grab rail between the ladder styles at floor level.*

(Geoffrey Ellis, June 1964; © 1996)

There was a spur on the miners tramway on a flat area just south of South Heighton Post Office Stores where Nos. 1 & 2 Brands Close now stand. This carried materials for the construction of the observation post. The track turned north when it reached the road, passing in front of the Post Office and continuing to a concealed and camouflaged area now occupied by Nos. 1 & 2 Manor Farm Cottages where the spoil was transferred into more dumpers, and building materials were reloaded onto the trucks to be transported to the pillbox sites.

Using this miner's tramway avoided the creation of tell-tale vehicle tracks in the downland pasture which would have invited unwelcome attention from enemy aerial reconnaissance. Considerable tonnages of marine ballast, cement, and iron reinforcement were thus moved across the hillside with minimal disturbance to the appearance of the downland pasture.

On completion of the constructional work, these tramways were dismantled and the west, south, and east facing slopes of Heighton hillside were fenced off with a 6ft (2m) high barbed-wire barricade which ran from behind Hampden Gardens in South Heighton to where Denton school now stands.

Finally, there was an externally accessed and independent semi-submerged pillbox at the western entrance at road level. This was designed to cover road borne assaults from the south or north, or frontal approaches from the west. A toilet block with conventional WCs and wash basins was built above the pillbox early in 1944 by the Duke of Cornwall's Light Infantry although this was demolished after the war. The concrete floor and glazed earthenware soil pipes are still in evidence in 1996.

*The derelict western entrance showing the two flights of steps and handrails in 1964. The flat area in front of the portal formed a rail head for a miners tramway during excavation. Near right is the thick concrete roof of the half submerged pillbox defending the tunnel entrance. A toilet block was built on this roof by the Duke of Cornwall's Light Infantry.*

(Geoffrey Ellis, June 1964; © 1996)

*External view of room 16. The tunnel entrance lies directly beneath the notice which formerly read "DRIVE SLOWLY". The concrete base of a former radio mast lies a yard from the utility cabinet. The original sea views are apparent from this picture.*

(Geoffrey Ellis, 11 December 1992)

Additional approach defences included 40-gallon fuel drums buried on their sides in the steep roadside bank to the south of the western entrance which could have been ignited to create walls of fire across the road melting the tarmac surface.

## Aerial Masts & Antennae

The aerial field occupied a site which is now Glynde Close. Three vertical iron pipes which rise 60ft (18m) through solid chalk from the operations centre carried the 0·5ins (12mm) diameter coaxial cables to a variety of antennae slung between tubular iron masts. Most masts (and there may have been up to a dozen) were 2ins in diameter and 26ft tall (0·05 x 8m) with two sets of three guy wires attached to the top and mid height. Dipoles and longwire antennae were strung between them. Official sources state that there were seven receiving and transmitting sets here, with provision for more. This type of antenna installation would have been very difficult to detect from the air since it cast no discernible shadows on the rough meadow grass.

At the western end of Denton House, just outside room 16, and straddling the tunnel, the tops of four concrete blocks were still prominent in 1996. The central concrete block had evidence of the former existence of a 3·5ins (88mm) diameter mast at its centre; the others were 23ft (7m) distant and well placed to have been anchors for guy wires. If a circle of 23ft (7m) radius was described about the central concrete block, radii described to the others would have formed 120° segments.

## Royal Engineers Officers Mess

Whilst South Heighton tunnels were under construction, a gabled house in Station Road, Bishopstone, served as office, store, and Officers Mess to the RE 172 Tunnelling Coy. Photographs of this building have been donated to Newhaven Fort by Mr William Wild, an Officer engaged there with Captain W Wilson, Officer in Charge.

## Post-war Abandonment

When the Naval decommissioned their Headquarters in the Guinness Trust Home on 31 August, 1945, and the other services withdrew from the tunnel, they performed a very thorough recovery of all the equipment, furniture and fittings.

Looters followed, aiming to salvage as much timber as possible, ripping the plywood lining from the tunnel walls to retrieve more than 9,000ft of timber battens used to support it leaving thousands of snipped wire ties dangling from the RSJs. The wooden cipher offices also disappeared without trace leaving only the painted lines on the flagstone flooring as a clue to their former existence fifty years later.

It was the eventual plundering of all this wooden battening which is responsible for the mass of rotting plywood and torn felt which exists on the floor today. Many breeze-block partitions were demolished where they obstructed access to this prized resource, proving beyond doubt that the tunnel lining was completed before the breeze-block partitions were built.

# HMS FORWARD SECURITY

Heighton Hill retained its secret throughout the war; only one bomb fell anywhere near, on ground now occupied by 29 St Martin's Crescent (then a fallow field), and it appears that was dropped indiscriminately one summer Sunday by an enemy aircraft being pursued by a Spitfire.

South Heighton's secret seems to have sustained elsewhere. There is no hint of this establishment in Duncan Campbell's *War Plan UK* (Paladin books ISBN 0-586-08479-7) nor Nigel West's book *GCHQ — The Secret Wireless War 1900–86* (Coronet books ISBN 0-340-41197-X). Both deal with subterranean military establishments, and were notoriously insensitive to the restricted information they revealed when first published.

HMS FORWARD's communication centre was 60ft below ground level and was (then) bomb proof. To destroy it would have required a direct assault — a matter which had not escaped the attentions of the designers! The lack of any attacks proves that it was unknown to the enemy. However, he did discover the name because Lord Haw-Haw once reported HMS FORWARD had been sunk!

Any assault successfully negotiating the mined beaches between Newhaven and Seaford, would not have arrived undetected. Comprehensive communications in the area ensured that a whole menu of defensive measures would have been alerted which included Bofers guns, tanks, searchlights, pillboxes, tank-traps and mined approach roads. HMS FORWARD had its own defences and in the unlikely event of reaching the tunnel, unpleasant surprises awaited the visitor.

Any attack on the Guinness Trust (east) end, would have involved entering the defended building and negotiating two substantial locked iron grilled gates after entering the tunnel, the second of which was half way down a flight of fifty-one stairs in full view of a heavily protected machine gun post. Attempts to silence this gun with hand grenades would have met with little success because of the gate, and a deep pit (normally covered) at the foot of the stairs into which any grenade would have rolled. Moreover, the blast from any explosion within the tunnel 50ft (15m) below ground level would have afflicted the attacker more than the defender. A massive armour plate door protected the operational centre.

At the west entrance, an externally accessed semi-submerged pillbox at road level defended any attack from the road or across the fields. The tunnel entrance had a strong close-grilled iron gate. Some twenty feet beyond the gate a heavily protected machine gun post was built into the tunnel wall, and the tunnel turned 45° to the left. The bend prevented firing into the tunnel had the machine gun been silenced. 20ft beyond the bend was a second grilled iron security gate. Some 100yds (90m) into the tunnel, another massive armour plate door protected the operational centre.

## Responsibility for the Protection of the tunnel

Having described the internal arrangements for the protection of HMS FORWARD, the remainder of this chapter will concentrate on the arguments establishing responsibilities for the provision of guards to defend establishment.

At first in 1941/2 the tunnel was defended by members of the South Heighton Home Guard. In an interview with the late Clem Butler regarding his Home Guard service with HMS FORWARD, Clem told me . . .

> *"I was nineteen when I joined the Home Guard at South Heighton. I lived in Hampden Gardens then. One of our responsibilities was night time guard duty in the pillboxes of the tunnel under Heighton Hill. I suppose there was four of us in each pillbox. We were inside those pillboxes all night. Oh my god, talk about dark, because you couldn't have a light, you couldn't smoke; you just had the machine gun sticking out. We used to have to stop in there all night long till the next morning.*

*"Our machine guns and ammunition were all stored in the old church hall (Formerly St Martin's, South Heighton). Every time we went on duty we had to take them from there, down the hill, and in the bottom entrance. They had a sealed door down in the tunnel. When we got to this sealed door we had to go up wooden steps. We weren't allowed past the armour plate door.*

*"I know when we first went in, and we looked up those steps, it looked a heck of a way up. There wasn't even any lights on the staircase for us; you had to go up by torchlight. You weren't allowed to put a light on up there anyway because anybody could see you from outside.*

*"We had four Vickers machine guns; of course we had to carry the guns right up those ruddy steps to the top. I remember lugging that gun up there; we had a handrail to hang on to, and then the last piece was straight up about nine feet. I was a lot younger then. Nothing was ever left in the tunnel, it was always brought back out. We also carried our own rifles; but we took them home."*

Sid Berry, another Homeguard member with a 'reserved occupation', remembers having to defend the tunnel 'for about a year whilst the Navy got its act together. We never got to see anything in there — we weren't allowed, and when we left we were told that we had never been there!'

The authorities were happy with this situation until the arrival of Admiralty letter M014220/42 dated 30 November, 1942, detailing the requirements for guarding Admiralty property. The following extracts from PRO file ADM1/13106 reveal an incredible chain of claim and counter-claim regarding the status of HMS FORWARD in correspondence from 4 December, 1942, to 17 September, 1943, pertaining to the interpretation of information contained in Admiralty letters and the eventual outcome.

ADM1/13106. NEWHAVEN Naval Headquarters, Protection of. Information re new arrangements 1943.

SECRET MEMO from NOIC NEWHAVEN. 4 December, 1942. Ref 016/425. To Commander in Chief, PORTSMOUTH.

With reference to Admiralty letter M014220/42 dated 30 November, 1942, paragraph 2, it is submitted that Their Lordships may be informed that the service personnel at the Naval Headquarters NEWHAVEN, apart from the Officers on the staff of the Naval Officer in Charge and sufficient ratings to provide one sentry on the door in four watches, consist entirely of WRNS ratings who are not accommodated in the building.

2. Unless it is proposed to provide a force from Naval sources capable of defending the isolated Headquarters against direct assault by the enemy, it is essential that this protection should be an Army commitment.

3. It is unquestionable that NOIC's Headquarters falls under the Grade "A" category mentioned in Admiralty letter MLD039062/42 dated 23 October, 1942, paragraph 2(c) for the following reasons

(a) contains terminal equipment for telephone lines to ten RDF stations which feed both the Naval and Canadian Corps Coastal Artillery Plots. The Combined Headquarters of the NEWHAVEN Sub-command and the Corps Coastal Artillery are situated in the tunnel beneath the Naval Headquarters. The information from the RDF stations feeding the NEWHAVEN plot is essential to the Commander-in-Chief PORTSMOUTH and to some extent the Vice-Admiral Dover. Both these authorities rely upon obtaining this information from NOIC's Headquarters.

(b) in addition to the above, the following telephone and communications are installed at Naval Headquarters.

Switchboards for Coastal Forces Base and local Naval telephones.

Terminal equipment for telephone lines to

    C-in-C PORTSMOUTH

    Vice-Admiral DOVER

RAF UXBRIDGE
Various Army Units in Canadian Corps area including Corps HQ
Resident Naval Officer SHOREHAM
Resident Naval Officer LITTLEHAMPTON
HMS VERNON (ROEDEAN)
HMS NEWT (NEWHAVEN — west side)
HMS LIZARD (to come)
BEACHY HEAD Signals station
(c) terminal equipment of three four-channel teleprinter systems.
(d) terminal equipment of telephone control lines of Corps Coastal Artillery and teleprinter.
(e) W/T station of seven transmitting and receiving sets. This number to be increased and control lines to additional distant sets to be fitted.
(f) Telephone lines to control posts from QL and SF sites in the neighbourhood of NEWHAVEN.
4. It would appear that Their Lordships cannot yet be fully aware of the importance of NOIC's Headquarters NEWHAVEN in both offensive and defensive roles or of the extent of the disaster involved in the destruction of the extensive communications system which has been, and is still being built up there.

*Signed Hardman-Jones. Captain RN. 7 December, 1942. C-in-C PORTSMOUTH.*

Appendix No. 7260/0/9872/10 to The Secretary of The Admiralty with a copy to the NEWHAVEN Naval Officer-in-Charge, NEWHAVEN.
Forwarded for the consideration of Their Lordships.
2. It is strongly urged that the Vulnerable Points Adviser should visit these Headquarters at an early date as previously required in paragraph 5(b) of PORTSMOUTH 6212/1872/10 of 2 November, 1942, in order that the whole matter may be put on a satisfactory basis.

*Signature resembles RJ DUKE for Admiral. 26 December, 1942.*

From C-in-C PORTSMOUTH (ref 7260/0/9872/10). Date 26/12/42. Subject. Defence of Naval Headquarters NEWHAVEN recommending visit of Vulnerable Points Adviser. (NOIC NEWHAVEN 016/45 4/12/42).
    Note. M014220/42 has been attached and C-in-C PORTSMOUTH's message 1851/29/12 inserted. Referred. RA MCARTHY 30/12/42.
    PORTSMOUTH's 1851/29 December, is the first intimation received in the Admiralty that the Army have been providing guards at NEWHAVEN Naval Headquarters. The arrangement must have been purely a local affair.
2. No reason is seen to alter the statement made in para 2 of Admiralty letter M014220/42 dated 30 November, which said that the specific local protection of Naval Headquarters as distinct from the general defence of the area is the responsibility of the service personnel of the establishment.
3. The further out letter from the Admiralty dated 29 December, giving C-in-C Home Forces remarks on the protection of NEWHAVEN has crossed NOIC NEWHAVEN's reply dated 4 December, to the earlier Admiralty letter. NOIC NEWHAVEN is still insisting on his Headquarters being listed as a Vulnerable Point and moreover as a Grade "A" Vulnerable Point which means "a point, the destruction of which might disastrously affect the course of the war."
4. As previously stated it is not the principle to classify Naval Headquarters as GHQ(VP). It so happened that the V.P.A. visited NEWHAVEN on 1 December, 1942, and inspected the Naval Headquarters. In his opinion adequate protection against sabotage will be provided by a guard on the main gate as the bulk of communications system is underground. The V.P.A. confirms the classification of the Headquarters as a GHQ(VP) is not justified.
5. With regard to para 4 in NOIC NEWHAVEN's letter dated 4 December, the importance of his

Headquarters is fully appreciated. At the same time C-in-C Home Forces has stated in para 3 of his letter HF11537/1/Ops of 15 December, 1942, that it is not a likely raid objective. This statement has not been disputed by the Admiralty. Admittedly, NOIC NEWHAVEN's Headquarters are in an isolated position but it is considered that its defence against "direct assault by the enemy" should be covered by the general dispositions of troops within the military command.

6. Submitted for approval to send the following signal to C-in-C PORTSMOUTH and NOIC NEWHAVEN. "Your 1851A(29 December) Admiralty letter M14220/42 of 29 December, 1942, refers. The Vulnerable Points Adviser inspected NEWHAVEN Naval HQ on 1 December, 1942, and does not consider the HQ should be included in the GHQ(VP) list. In his opinion adequate protection against sabotage will be provided by a guard on the main door. Disposition of troops to provide protection against direct assault by the enemy is the responsibility of the local military commander."

7. After action it is proposed that M Branch should send an explanatory letter in the sense of the above minute to C-in-C PORTSMOUTH.

*Signed SK Bain for Director of Local Defence. 31 December, 1942.*

PINK DOCUMENT. SECRET Message 1851A/29 December. IN.

From C-in-C PORTSMOUTH 29/12/42. PL by TP received 2128. Addressed Admiralty, repeated NOIC NEWHAVEN. IMPORTANT. 516 reference PORTSMOUTH No. 6212/9872/10 2 November, Admiralty letter M014220/42 of 30 November and PORTSMOUTH minute No. 7260/0/9872/10 of 26 December.

Information now received that Army withdrawing guard on Naval Headquarters and Base NEWHAVEN on 7 January. Request urgent representation be made to change to Home Forces that present guards be retained on Headquarters and Base until whole question has been examined by VP Adviser as already proposed in my minute quoted above. 29 December.

WHITE DOCUMENT. SECRET Message 1059A/1 January. OUT.

To C-in-C PORTSMOUTH 996 NOIC NEWHAVEN 1/1/43. Secret cipher. From Admiralty. Your 1851/29 December, Admiralty letter M014220/42 of 29 December, 1942, refers.

2. The Vulnerable Points Adviser inspected NEWHAVEN Naval HQ on 1 December, 1942, and does not consider that the HQ should be included in the GHQ(VP) list. In his opinion adequate protection against sabotage will be provided by a guard on the main door.

3. Disposition of troops to provide protection against direct assault by the enemy is the responsibility of the local military commander.

PINK DOCUMENT. SECRET Message 1925A/4 January. IN.

From C-in-C PORTSMOUTH 4/1/43 Received 2135 PL by A.T.X. Addressed Admiralty, repeated NOIC NEWHAVEN. 627.

Admiralty message 1059/1 NOIC NEWHAVEN. informs me that on 1 December, 1942, his Headquarters were visited by Captain BURTON of the War Office, but this visit was understood to be solely connected with the protection of RDF stations. Protection of NEWHAVEN Headquarters was not discussed by Captain BURTON with any Naval Officer. It is not known therefore whether he was cognisant of the strategic value of these Headquarters. As a matter of fact we do not agree that a guard on the door is adequate protection against sabotage as there are other means of access and control of the western entrance to the tunnel is necessary.

I am much concerned regarding the security of NEWHAVEN Naval Base including the Harbour and Headquarters from the point of view of a surprise raid as opposed to the defence of NEWHAVEN in the case of invasion. PORTSMOUTH's mission 6212/9872/10 of 2 November, 1942, endeavours to set out the risk to NEWHAVEN from a raid. My experience has shown me that NEWHAVEN is of great strategic value for the operation of coastal craft against enemy vessels making the Straits of DOVER and proceeding to the West by the French shore. For this purpose it is necessary to make use of

NEWHAVEN as an advanced base for the coastal striking forces. These cannot be operated from PORTSMOUTH for this purpose without long periods on patrol which is impracticable owing to lack of reliability of these craft and maintenance routines. The Base repair facilities at NEWHAVEN are therefore an essential feature in the operation of the striking force. Unless Their Lordships can inform me therefore that the defence against a surprise raid is now unnecessary, I must press for a local garrison of guard vide para 5 of my letter quoted above which would be able to hold the Harbour, Base and Headquarters until reinforcements arrive.

I suggest therefore with reference to para 3 of APM014220/42 of 30 November, 1942, that Their Lordships should represent this point of view to the War Office and C-in-C Home Forces. It is clear from the letter from Naval Officer-in-Charge that this garrison or guard cannot be provided from local Naval resources.

SECRET letter dated 12 January, 1943. M016455/42.

To the C-in-C PORTSMOUTH, Copy to Naval Officer-in-Charge, NEWHAVEN ref No. 016/425 of 4 December, 1942.

With reference to various messages herein quoted, I am to forward the following further remarks on the question of the protection of NEWHAVEN Base and Naval Headquarters.

2. There are two separate points at issue. Firstly the garrisoning of the Base which automatically ensures the protection of the Naval Headquarters against raids, and secondly the specific local protection of the Naval Headquarters against sabotage.

3. The first is the responsibility of the Commander-in-Chief Home Forces working through the local military commander and is no way the concern of the Vulnerable Points Adviser. The second is the responsibility of the local Naval authority.

3. The Commander-in-Chief Home Forces is aware of the Naval importance of NEWHAVEN as the Admiralty stressed this point when asking him to comment on your letter No. 6212/9872/10 dated 2 November, 1942. In his reply to the Admiralty letter the Commander-in-Chief Home Forces stated that "the protection of the port of NEWHAVEN is a general operational matter and has been taken into account in relation to other factors when determining the disposition of troops." Included in these factors must be warning of raids to be expected from such sources as RDF, coastal patrols, and coastal watchers.

4. The Commander-in-Chief Home Forces has now forwarded the following information
   (a) NEWHAVEN itself is a garrison
   (b) Stationed in NEWHAVEN, there is one Battalion Infantry and one Coast Regiment Royal Artillery.
   (c) At SEAFORD, two miles to the Eastward, there is an Infantry Brigade HQ, one Battalion Infantry, and one Army Tank Battalion.
   (d) At DENTON, about three quarters of a mile North-East of NEWHAVEN there is one Infantry Battalion.
   (e) At WEST FIRLE about four miles North-East of NEWHAVENthere is one Field Regiment Royal Artillery.
   (f) At ROTTINGDEAN, six miles West of NEWHAVEN, there is the Headquarters of an Army Tank Brigade.

5. In making his dispositions against hostile raids the Commander-in-Chief Home Forces has to reduce the forces employed on static defence to the limit of safety in order to provide the maximum number of men to train for offensive operations.

6. In regard to the security of the Naval Headquarters against sabotage, and it's listing as a Vulnerable Point, it is not the accepted policy to list Naval Headquarters as GHQ Vulnerable Points. It is generally found possible to arrange for the personnel normally employed in the Headquarters or the Base to afford sufficient protection.

7. Their Lordships cannot agree with the statement by the Naval Officer-in-Charge NEWHAVEN in paragraph 3 of his submission to the Commander-in-Chief PORTSMOUTH dated 4 December, 1942, that "it is unquestionable that the Naval Officer-in-Charge's Headquarters falls under the Grade 'A' category."

8. That a military guard has been provided heretofore for the Naval Headquarters is not previously known to the Admiralty and was presumably arranged locally. It is assumed that this guard was part of the disposition of troops by the military commander against direct assault by the enemy.

9. In order to meet your request for a visit by the Vulnerable Points Adviser the Admiralty will make a request for him to visit personally your Headquarters by command of Their Lordships.
   *HN MORRISON.*

Letter from The Grange, BEACONSFIELD, Bucks. 21 February, 1943. Telephone BEACONSFIELD 1175. Reference VPA/323/A/5. SECRET.

Sir, In confirmation of opinions expressed during a recent visit to the RN Base Headquarters NEWHAVEN, the following remarks are recorded.

(a) The introduction of Royal Marines or RMP into the Base HQ in lieu of the Army guard which is shortly to be withdrawn is essential. The HQ establishment as it stands at present is quite unable to undertake any comprehensive security task. The tunnel portion of the Headquarters being a vital feature, the above guards should be employed thereon and I suggest a single sentry by day and a double sentry by night on each entrance. To assist security I advise the introduction of a second iron gate at each entrance which can be closed immediately in an emergency by the second sentry acting in support of the first, and if possible hidden from immediate view.

A system of alarms for local and tunnel to surface purposes would be an asset. Sabotage of either type being the most likely contingency, I advise the removal of existing camouflage at the tunnel entrance which at present only serves to draw attention to the latter. The present arrangements for the scrutiny and check of individuals seeking entrance into the building are satisfactory and a post at the outer gate is not essential. This however should be closed all night if possible, and reliance placed on a patrol inside the building where access in default of barred windows etc is a simple matter. Anything which can be done to restrict entry or limit the possibility is worthy of consideration. Other Naval interests within the Base, namely magazines (one inch map ref: 134/883207) and petrol both in the port (134/882198) and in the quarry area can be supervised economically and efficiently by RN personnel in the vicinity, and it is unlikely that guards as a permanent feature will be found to be necessary. As regards petrol and oil, fire fighting and watching arrangements appear to be sufficiently comprehensive already. It would be advantageous to insist on the maximum amount of control activity consistent with fire duties in general as an anti-petty sabotage measure. Pumping gear and valves constitute vulnerable features. The arming of men so employed deserves consideration, but this is not a vital matter. The magazines and contents are not considered to constitute a sufficiently attractive target for sabotage and the risks of theft and demolition can be discounted.

Sabotage by stealth which might take the form of tampering with fuses, etc, is best countered by intermittent supervision during the hours of darkness and provision of suitable locking devices.

Buildings are particularly strong, but the present bars and padlocks on doors are no obstacle. It is suggested that these be reinforced and the actual hasp and padlock countersunk in cement in order to prevent use of tools as a means of effecting quick entry.

I am, Sir, your obedient servant,
*Signed by CLARKE Brigadier, Vulnerable Points Adviser.*

SECRET DOCUMENT from the VPA. Ref. VPA/323/A/5. Dated 21/2/43. Subject: RN Base Headquarters NEWHAVEN — Recommendations regarding protection.

The attached letter results from a personal inspection of NEWHAVEN Naval Headquarters by Brigadier CLARKE jointly with AD of LD CI to C-in-C PORTSMOUTH and NOIC NEWHAVEN.

2. Anti-sabotage protection of the NEWHAVEN Headquarters has been accepted as a Naval responsibility and it is considered that RM Police are the most suitable type for this commitment. AGRM referred.

3. Before action by AGRM Head of M is requested forward a copy of the VPA's letter to C-in-C

PORTSMOUTH, copy to NOIC NEWHAVEN for information and action as necessary and to inform him that the recommendation in para (a) first sentence of the VPA's letter is under consideration.

*Signed GE Johnson Director for Local Defence. 24 February, 1943.*

Post-script to this letter RMP 87/7/43.

Neither Royal Marine Police nor Admiralty Civil Police are at present available in this locality and are unlikely to materialise. It has been represented on another paper (USB1384/42) by the Chief Constable that the Royal Marine Guard of one Corporal and nine Marines are no longer required at the RN Torpedo Factory at Greenock, and if and when their withdrawal is approved it is proposed to arrange for them to be transferred to NEWHAVEN.

*Signed by the Adjutant General Royal Marines, March, 1943.*

Further minute, register No. M02040/43 on USB1384/42 which D of LD has now seen, approval has been given to increase the RM Police compliment at RNTF Greenock thereby rendering the RM Guard redundant. It is understood that AGRM is making arrangements to withdraw the RM guard. Will AGRM please indicate when it will be available for duty at NEWHAVEN.

*Signature unreadable, Director of Local Defence. 14 March, 1943.*

Over-leaf reads . . . RM No. 8289/43A2 As the guard at Greenock has served there since 1939, it is intended to withdraw the personnel and send a new guard to NEWHAVEN on 1 April, 1943.

*Signed by the Adjutant General RM. 23 March, 1943.*

Reply noted. Will Head of M inform C-in-C PORTSMOUTH and NOIC NEWHAVEN further to our letter of 27/2/43 in the following sense.

1. A Royal Marine guard will be provided for the Base HQ as from 1 April, 1943.
2. The other recommendations in para 1 of the VPA's letter should be implemented and a report of the measures taken forwarded in due course.

*Signed LE JOHNSON for Director of Local Defence. 25 March, 1943.*

Reference sheet The Captain GIBBENS in manuscript on the top, dated 26 March, 1943. To D of LD NEWHAVEN.

With reference to D of LD's minute, dated 15 March, 1943, arrangements have been made with the War Department to take over the following accommodation for Naval guard.

(a) Old Chapel, NEWHAVEN
(b) No. 7 South View Terrace, NEWHAVEN
(c) Brighthaven, Denton Rise, NEWHAVEN
(d) No. 2 Southdown Cottages, NEWHAVEN

*Signed W BOYDD for Chief and Surveyor of Lands.*

SECRET MEMO: Subject Defence of NEWHAVEN. From C-in-C PORTSMOUTH. 4 August, 1943. No. 3914/0/0115/89.

To Secretary of the Admiralty, Copy to NOIC, NEWHAVEN. With reference to the Admiralty letter M02040/43 of 29 March, 1943, be pleased to inform Their Lordships that the following recommendations specified in the Vulnerable Points Advisers' No. 323/A/5 of 21 February, 1943, have now been carried out.

(a) The guard at the Headquarters now consists of one Corporal, and nine Marines and one Petty Officer, one Leading Seaman, and eight LDD Ratings.
(b) A system of alarm circuits has now been fitted.
(c) The existing camouflage has been removed, and the entrance to the tunnel made less obvious by turfing and painting.
(d) The padlocks of the doors of the magazines have been cemented and strengthened and are now considered secure.

2. The fitting of a second iron gate at each entrance has been delayed but the estimate for the erection of these two gates has now been approved and the gates will be fitted next month. One Corporal and nine Marines who have been sent as a guard are insufficient to provide the sentries as recommended by the Vulnerable Points Adviser in his letter VPA323/A/5 of 21 November, 1943. This necessitated supplying one Petty Officer, one Leading Seaman and eight LDD Ratings especially from PORTSMOUTH. This matter has formed a proposal made by Admiral BINNEY after visiting NEWHAVEN that the Naval part of the guard be abolished and one Sergeant, one Corporal and four Marines be substituted who together with the previous numbers will be adequate. This is fully concurred in.

    *C LAURELSLITTLE (?) Admiral.*

    Noted. Approval to replace one Petty Officer, one Leading Seaman, and eight LDD Ratings by one Sergeant, one Corporal, and four Marines for guard duties has already been given by the Board. ALM07477/43 of 9 August, 1943, to C-in-C PORTSMOUTH refers.

    Signed LE JOHNSON. Director of Local Defence. 13 August, 1943.

Note RM No. 8289/43A3.

    One Sergeant, one Corporal, and four Marines are available and arrangements have been made for them to be provided by CHATHAM Division RM. The guard of One Corporal and nine Marines was provided by this Division. It is assumed the complement will be amended in due course. AGRM has not seen papers M07477/43 and it is requested that papers of this nature may in future be referred to AGRM before a decision is taken to ascertain whether Royal Marines are available.

    *Signed H RICHES for Lt-Col. AGRM 3 September, 1943.*

SECRET REPLY. 17 September. Commander-in-Chief PORTSMOUTH, copy to NOIC NEWHAVEN.

    With reference to your submission of 3914/0/0115/89 of 4 August, 1943, and to Admiralty letter M07477/43 of 9 August, I am to acquaint you that arrangements have been made for one Sergeant, one Corporal and four Marines to be provided by CHATHAM Division RM in substitution for the Naval guard at the Base Headquarters NEWHAVEN. The arrangements made to implement the Vulnerable Points Advisers other recommendations have been noted.

    *By command of Their Lordships, JGN ALLCOCK.*

## End of PRO extracts

WH Taylor ex-RN told me that he carried out guard duties at the western end of the tunnel, and also manned the Lewis gun which was mounted in a sandbagged circle "in front of the large house" from 5 March, 1943, to 5 August, 1943. His guard room was No. 7 Southview, and he was billeted in a cottage (formerly Southdown Cottages) next door to the Hampden Arms pub. His messdeck was "a flint built barn type building opposite our billets" (the Old Chapel). These are the properties mentioned above.

# A WREN TELEGRAPHIST REMEMBERS

The Womens Royal Naval Service (WRNS) provided the largest contingent serving in the tunnel. WRNS Telegraphist 85486 Marguerite Humphreys (now Curtis) kindly supplied a most comprehensive pen-picture of her view of service life with HMS FORWARD from a wide variety of angles.

*"All WRNS had to have passed the School Certificate which, in those days, meant you HAD to pass in English language, Arithmetic, and one foreign language (French in my case). Even if you passed with distinction in any amount of other subjects, if you failed one of the set requirements, you had to sit the whole lot again — no picking and choosing, or carrying forward your better pass marks.*

Marguerite Humphreys

*"I trained at HMS CABBALA, Lowton St Mary's, Leigh, Lancashire. This was a six months course and we had to pass out in six subjects — Procedure; Coding; Receiving; Transmitting; Technical; and Theory. We were trained to transmit and receive at 24–25 words per minute, but the pass mark speed at the end of the course was 20wpm. Believe you me, you never forget Morse. It creeps up on you at most unexpected times and you find yourself di-da-ing tapping out or transcribing letters and figures into Morse. I always had a bit of a mental block in distinguishing "H" from "5" when we were receiving mixed letters and figures causing me a great deal of anguish. We had various phrases which transcribed rhythmically into Morse and we used to practice them over and over again; one was beef essence. We had to be able to receive in French (with the various accents as well as the language). At the end of March 1944, after completing this course, three of us were sent to HMS FORWARD.*

*"I remember HMS FORWARD particularly for its long steep descent into the bowels of the earth. There was a heavy metal door; and half way down there was a machine-gun post with a barrel pointing up the stairs.*

"At that time a three watch system was being worked, and we were each assigned to a watch. I cannot now remember the sequence of how the watches were matched to the days, but over a three day period the watches were divided 0800 to noon, noon to 1600, 1600 to 2000 (the dog watches), and 2000 to 0800 the following morning (night watch). Before our arrival there was a Leading WRNS Telegraphist and two WRNS Telegraphists on each watch — we increased each complement by one.

"There were also two civilians in their late 40s/50s, known as Uncle Alf and Uncle Stu. They lived locally and had been Wireless Officers on the Newhaven-Dieppe Cross Channel boats pre-1939. They were there during the day. Supervising us was Chief Petty Officer Nobby Clark and three-badge Leading Hand Clasby. Both lived locally.

"The civilian (Uncle Alf or Uncle Stu), the CPO, or the Leading Hand, whoever was in charge overall, had a direct line (by buzzer) to either Portsmouth or Newhaven which they used if any 'immediate' or 'urgent' signal was received; alternatively 'they' got in touch with FORWARD.

"The callsign of HMS FORWARD was MFF and we double-banked Portsmouth whose callsign was MTN; Dover's callsign was MTU, which was double-banked by Ramsgate, callsign MFK. In the case of PORTSMOUTH being 'knocked out' we would have taken over. We received and recorded all messages on their wavelengths and, on occasions, transmitted on their behalf. In the first few weeks I was at FORWARD (those weeks prior to D-Day), all signal traffic was largely connected with exercises taking place in the Channel and offshore etc. These signals were distinguished by the inclusion of — X — in the preamble.

"We always used Morse, and Naval code which consisted of a five-figure block, then the message in four-figure blocks, ending with the five figure block. (On D-Day night, a new code was used — AQUA code — the first block was AQUA then three or four letter blocks — this was broken by the Germans in a day or two and was abandoned). The Germans frequently jammed the frequencies, particularly the Portsmouth frequency.

Picture Postcard of Surrey House, Seaford, used as Wrennery.

S. 247a (Established June, 1933, Revised A[ ]g., 1934)   H.M.S. FORWARD

SURNAME

HuMPHREYS

CHRISTIAN NAME(S)

MARGUE[ ]

O.N. 8 5 4 x [ ]

RATING   WREN

G. or T.   CPO

(214)   Wt. 41613/D6229   220M   ( [ ]rts)   2/41   S.E.R. Ltd.   Gp. 671.

WAT_H
PART

PART OF
[ ]S  SHIP  S .H.[ ]

[ ]P.B.[ ]
MESS

RELIGION

*Surrey House Pass.*

"Just before D-Day there was an intake of male Telegraphists — three Leading Hands (Phil Sherwood, Frank Hands, Tommy Gorman) and Telegraphists, of whom I remember Vic Sievey, Bob Laidlaw, Reg Cannan and several others. They were experienced sea-going men who had been on Russian or Atlantic convoys. They had worked watch and watch about (four hours on and four hours off for months on end) so FORWARD was a haven for them. All the men were billeted in Denton or South Heighton.

"I was on watch the day scheduled for D-Day, but it was postponed for 24 hours because of bad weather. Before going off watch the Commodore spoke to us all emphasising we must _not_ speak even among ourselves, of what we had seen and heard in the tunnel. We were all very solemn that night as we strolled along Seaford seafront; the sea was really wild. Shortly after D-Day we became very busy and the signals room was a hive of activity.

"When on night watch (2000 to 0800 the next morning), we snatched a quarter of an hour as a break for sandwiches, tea, and a trip to the 'heads'; but if it was slack we would take turns off for an hour or two and put our heads down in the sleeping quarters (about four or six bunks in each room, one room for men, another for WRNS). There was a 'kitchen' in the tunnel where tea could be made. During the day, I recall a person called Grace who wielded a big metal teapot, but at night time you made your own for the watch. "What I do remember is the fuggy airless pong (no other word for it) of the tunnel. Now a trip to the 'heads' entailed going through heavy metal doors with a long walk 'through the hill' to the bottom entrance where there was a lone Marine sentry on guard and two loos outside. A bit embarrassing for us, but it must have been a welcome break for him to have a chat — but the breath of fresh air after the tunnel was wonderful.

"My only experience 'up top' was coming on and off watch, and on Pay Day when we lined up, the Paymaster and his Writer at a table. We approached, saluted, gave our name and number, received our pay, saluted again, and walked away smartly. I think we received £2/10s a fortnight (£2·50 in decimal money).

*Wrens from HMS FORWARD took part in a Squad Drill competition at HMS VERNON (Roedean College) 1944. Anon.*
(Geoffrey Ellis, 1944; © 1996)

"The WRNS who were already at FORWARD when we arrived were quartered at Denton, whereas we were quartered at Seaford in Surrey House. This had been a men's convalescent home — an Edwardian building, lovely views, set in its own grounds. The disadvantage was the size of the rooms which we used as cabins (dormitories). One I was in slept twenty-four (six double bunks on each side, like a hospital ward). As we were mainly watchkeepers on differing watches, sometimes it was difficult to sleep during the day with all the comings and goings, radios on, chatter, etc.

"Each cabin rented a radio from a shop in Seaford for about 1s/6d or 2s/0d a week (8–10p in new money although considerably more in real terms), for which we all chipped in our share. It was more or less permanently tuned to the American Forces Network (except for BBC News and ITMA). Many of the girls had someone close in the Services (RAF, Naval, Army — a husband, fiancé, brother or parent). Some were POWs or posted as missing so they would listen daily to Lord Haw-Haw's broadcasts from Germany — 'Germany calling, Germany calling' — they did this as he would give long lists of POWs, wounded, or bodies found etc (as well as a whole load of disinformation) like when he announced that HMS FORWARD had been sunk!

"During the warm summer days of 1944 we would come off nightwatch, grab blankets and pillows, and find somewhere in the garden to sleep. We always 'looked out' for one another making sure we woke in time for lunch or a 'date'. Some girls would really sunbathe — stripping down to the bare necessities but this was suddenly stopped. There was a Polish Fighter Squadron at Polegate — when they came back from a sortie over the Channel, they diverted off course and flew low over Surrey House to view the bathing belles. Their CO got in touch with our WRNS Officer and we were all told to be more circumspect.

"A greater proportion of the WRNS quartered at Seaford worked for NOIC Newhaven — Boatscrew, Torpedo WRNS, Artificers, as well as the Writers etc. A motley crew, you might say — they were certainly a mixed bunch both in age and background. I remember Lavender Herbert who was the daughter of APH Herbert (the author and columnist) — there was an older person (Masie) who was a gifted artist, a Bishop's daughter, several daughters of Admirals, and University graduates. It was certainly an education in the University of Life for me and my friend Irene, who came from a sleepy

*HMS FORWARD Wrens relax at Seaford, August 1944. Joan Crew; Peggy Martin; Marguerite Curtis; Irene Lewis; Nancy Longstaff; & Anon.*

(Tom Bonnor; © 1993)

county town on the borders of England and Wales. (Irene and I were at school together from the age of ten; we joined the WRNS together, were at FORWARD together, and remained the closest of friends until sadly she died in 1991).

"The WRNS who worked in Newhaven were bussed to and from watch. The bus would pick us all up, stopping at various points in Seaford. We would go to Newhaven, and then on to Denton. The bus would wait for those coming off watch, back to Newhaven to pick up those coming off watch there, then back to Seaford. I must say we enjoyed being at Seaford, there was more to do off watch — a cinema, a good canteen in the town centre, the Scotch Tea Rooms, and another café on the front. The more sophisticated joined the Canadian Army Officers at the Pelham Club. There was the convenience of the railway station, so we could get to Brighton on our days free.

"A favourite jaunt was to get the Eastbourne bus to Exceat Farm, walk over High-and-Over hill to Alfriston, tea at The Urn or Druscillas (where occasionally we could get a boiled egg!), and then bus back again. We would walk over the Seven Sisters and got to know the various gun crews who always gave us tea and 'jelly pieces' (which I found out to be Bread and Jam). We would go to the Coastguard cottages on Beachy Head where the Royal Observer Corps had a lookout point. Again, always good for tea and a bite to eat. I have wonderful memories of warm summer days, the Downs, cowslips, poppies, harebells, and lizards (unknown in my part of the world).

"In February/March/April 1945 everything slackened, and talk was all 'when it's over'. Two at a time we exchanged places with WRNS Telegraphists from Fort SOUTHWICK, PORTSMOUTH, which had been the centre of all operations and planning for D-Day. I think we went for two to three weeks (to give the PORTSMOUTH WRNS a break). Whilst I was there I did have one moment whereby I felt I made a little bit of history. The whole of one watch, at half hourly intervals, I had to send out the Ultimatum (in plain language) to the Channel Islands, giving terms of surrender.

"I was on watch on VE Day and received the signal 'Splice the mainbrace'. That evening a gang of us went to Brighton and we sang and danced in the streets.

"In June, 1945, I was posted to the holding depot at Portsmouth and was demobbed in the September. My days at FORWARD were the most intense of my life. We lived and worked to the full extent of our abilities. It was really a terrible anticlimax when it was all over; civilian life was so different to our dreams. You missed the comradeship and the company. How sad it was to say 'Goodbye' to our watchmates as they were posted away. With all the good intentions in the world to keep in touch, and meet up again, in our heart of hearts we knew this would not be so, and it was 'Goodbye' to a phase in our lives."

# POST-WAR FORWARD

When the Admiralty abandoned the tunnel leaving the gate open, it left an open invitation for anybody to venture within. The labyrinth has attracted both young and old to explore its interior on account of the air of mystery which surrounds it.

As mentioned before, initial visitors liberated much material it contained, principally wood, copper wire and lead pipe. Some over ambitious salvagers who recovered a cable known to cross the valley meadows to the tunnel were unaware the cable still carried working telephone circuits. Cutting the cable advertised their unlawful business and led to their apprehension.

When I entered the tunnel in 1946, I had no understanding of what had happened there. Air-conditioning, trunking, and cable-tray in abundance exuded an impression of importance catching my imagination, determining me to discover more.

Many have ventured into the labyrinth since as names and dates recorded in the tunnel testify. One name, handwritten on a pillbox interior wall, unwittingly photographed in 1964, earned its author the displeasure of his father thirty years later when shown the picture, because the writer had always fervently denied ever having been in there!

Another local correspondent wrote: "I frequently used to explore the tunnel as a young lad with my friends, much to the chagrin of local residents and my fearsome headmistress, Miss Hooper, of South Heighton school. We always seemed to get caught by an irate adult who would follow us in and flush us out, which was most frustrating because I invariably got a thick ear from my father and the full force of Miss Hooper's savage tongue at school.

"Young lads had to 'prove' themselves by entering the bottom entrance armed with just a box of matches to counter the deathly oppressive blackness. The object was to creep (gingerly!) making your way up to the pillbox adjacent to the path leading down to the old reading room (now gone). Once in the pillbox, you had to squeeze through the gun ports and walk back down the track to rejoin your pals who would be waiting to see you did not emerge the way you went in. Only those who succeeded were considered men. I well recall the fear when a match was spent and you had to fumble for another in the awful blackness. Of course, the first time I tried this, the late Reverend Downs was passing as I came out."

The tunnel has had unwelcome attention from tramps and arsonists and some incidents have resulted in the attendance of the Fire Brigade and the Police. Mercifully, to my knowledge, there have been no serious accidents although potential hazards exist everywhere. The Local Authority which 'inherited' this establishment repeatedly sealed up the bottom entrance to discourage visitors from entering the tunnel, but masonry was no real deterrent to those lusting for adventure.

In the early 1970s, the hillside above the tunnel was sold to a developer who demolished the four pillboxes and the mock hen house. Much of the concrete hardcore produced was dumped into the access shafts. This removed the natural ventilation from the tunnel, and effectively sealed it. A 22yds (20m) length of the western access gallery was reinforced with masonry and liquid silica cement grout to support the weight of the surface development above. The developer had to remove the fall of chalk shown in my 1964 photographs of the western entrance to carry out this work. This provided another opportunity for adventurism.

The tunnel was subsequently resealed, and would-be visitors were discouraged by burying the external concrete steps with rubbish. Nature has since obscured the portal with dense undergrowth and overgrowth.

## Conclusion

HMS FORWARD Naval Headquarters earned an unpublicised place in history. It must now be recognised posthumously for its roles in the War of the Channel, the Dieppe Raid, the Normandie

Landings, and the Liberation of France. Similar establishments at Dover and Portsmouth have not been allowed to deteriorate in ignominy.

Time and progress has erased much evidence of this tunnel's existence, which is a pity; for it is as much part of our National Heritage as any other Ancient Monument. Seventy-four Martello Towers were built circa 1800 to counter a Napoleonic invasion which never happened. Although constructed to Defend the Realm, they were never used in anger, but have become part of our heritage.

Regrettably it is too late to preserve much of this establishment, but it is not too late to save what does remain for the education of generations to come, and as a tourist attraction. Whilst not suggesting that any part of the tunnel is structurally unsound, there must be merit in observing a responsible attitude towards preserving the residual fabric of the labyrinth, rather than the 'out of sight, out of mind' policy practised over the last fifty years. Regulated tourism could provide a solution, and may become a reality if proposals to declare the site an Ancient Monument are realised.

The information accumulated by this research must be retained for posterity as the only genuine sources of this material are disappearing. One ex-WRNS quipped "We are definitely an endangered species, but we are not extinct yet!"

Finally, an appeal. I would welcome any further information or reminiscences, however seemingly insignificant, pertaining to this establishment. Memories are the only source of unrecorded information — and these will not last for ever!

# THE GUINNESS TRUST HOLIDAY HOME

Before the war South Heighton had arable and dairy farms, a pub, a post office, a school and three dozen dwellings. The building of the Guinness Trust Holiday Home was the largest development in the village since the coming of the already redundant cement works.

The Guinness Trust Holiday Home was built by Ringmer Building Works in 1938; an architecturally pleasant building, it stood majestically on Heighton Hill looking down over virgin hillside to lush green meadows of the valley of the river Ouse, with views of Seaford Bay and the English Channel beyond. It was built to provide holiday accommodation for city-bound tenants of the London Guinness Trust Estates, and had sixteen dormitory apartments and a communal dining

*Entrance to Denton House showing the pleasant architectural appearance of the building, with room 16 at extreme right. The entrance was widened and lined with cobblestones, circa 1965.*

(Geoffrey Ellis, 11 December 1992)

*Classical view of Denton House showing the rear architectural appearance of the building. The sun terraces and lawns remained unaltered, but some glazing had been modernised. Room 16 at extreme left.*

(Geoffrey Ellis, 11 December 1992)

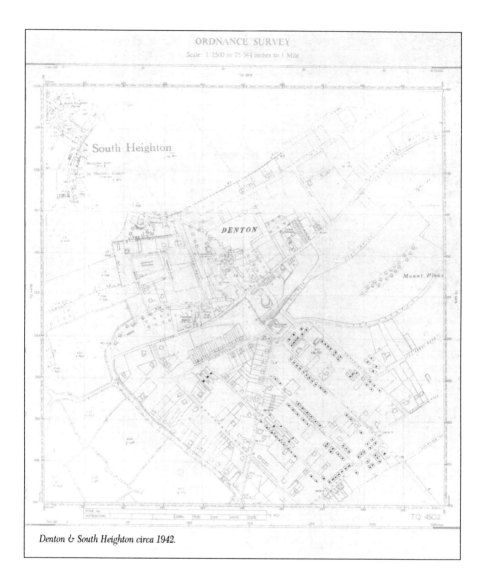

ORDNANCE SURVEY
Scale: 1:2500 or 25·344 inches to 1 Mile

South Heighton

DENTON

Mount Pleas

TQ 4502

*Denton & South Heighton circa 1942.*

room and sun lounge. Most apartments had access to a large sun terrace and lawn; and a private suite on the first floor housed a resident caretaker.

The clouds of war were already looming large when the Holiday Home opened for its first season, and the onset and development of Hitler's war put paid to all immediate prospects of holidays. The fall of Dunkirk and subsequent occupation of France by Germany prompted the Army to evict the Navy from the Sheffield Hotel, and the Admiralty to requisition the Guinness Trust Holiday Home from 20 June, 1940, for the 'duration'. Initially the Guinness Trust Holiday Home served as an administrative Naval HQ for the Newhaven sub-command. Suddenly, there was much to be done reorganising the sub-command and arranging additional maritime coastal protection of the Sussex coast with minefields and blockships.

*View of Dining Room 1961, showing mural.*

An external groundsman's machinery store about 18ft x 25ft (6 x 8m) in a basement beneath room 4 was adapted to provide protected accommodation before the commissioning of the tunnel at the end of 1941. Its already reinforced concrete ceiling was supplemented with three additional 8ins x 6ins (200 x 150mm) RSJs held in place by six very substantial pit props. Dennis Tompsett remembers these RSJs being cut to length by soldiers using a hacksaw! The provision of an emergency escape hatch to the outside world, and a 6ins (150mm) square cable hole into an internal passageway above the store suggest that a switchboard and emergency control centre was initially established here.

Following an Admiralty directive of March, 1941, requiring certain ports to maintain Naval plots, a subterranean operational centre resistant to assault by bombardment was designed and constructed. Sixty feet below ground, all the communications equipment required for intelligence gathering and dissemination was assembled. The principal operational entrance emerged into room 16 of the Guinness Trust Holiday Home from where one hundred and twenty two steps led down to an impenetrable underground fortress concealing some of the latest communications equipment available. No expense was spared in providing for almost every contingency likely to occur due to enemy action either by direct assault or failure of the public utilities.

As the Newhaven sub-command Headquarters, HMS FORWARD covered HMS MARLBOROUGH at Eastbourne, HMS AGGRESSIVE and HMS NEWT at Newhaven, HMS LIZARD at Hove, and Resident Naval Officers at Shoreham, and Littlehampton. Naval Stores depots were established at Lewes and Burgess Hill to supply permanent, consumable, and after action stores. Naval canteen service was organised for the area. Special Sick Quarters were requisitioned, and fully staffed and equipped and numerous large establishments were requisitioned locally and at Seaford to accommodate the WRNS. It is recorded that there were eventually over ten thousand Naval staff on HMS FORWARD 's ledgers.

HMS FORWARD was always commanded by a Captain (often, an Admiral serving in the rank of Captain) who occupied the upstairs caretakers' suite with its independent bathroom and cooking facilities. Lieut (Chad) Chadwick who served here in 1942 spoke of the honour of being invited to dine with the Captain in his quarters. Being a Naval Headquarters, the building had a large complement of RN and WRNS Officers so the Captain was never short of dinner guests.

During the Naval occupation a large semi-circular canvas was hung above the hall fireplace. A gifted serviceman painted a scene of Newhaven harbour circa 1900 depicting a cross-channel ferry amongst long masted sailing vessels. The canvas survived until 1965 when it was removed and destroyed whilst redecorating the hall for the WRVS. Unfortunately no known photographs exist of the painting alone, although it features as a backdrop in others.

A wartime Naval party undertaking a maritime investigation of Eastbourne pier is said to have 'found' a grand piano which, they considered, would store better in heated accommodation than the damp atmosphere at the end of the pier. When they returned, the piano accompanied them to the Guinness Trust Home!

An undated (but clearly wartime) copy of Ordnance Survey Map TQ4502 shows Denton, Mount Pleasant and South Heighton in detail (see page 86). All the Nissen huts and military buildings of the Army Transit Camp are plainly shown on Mount Pleasant, but the Guinness Trust Holiday Home has been carefully erased.

As far as the Admiralty was concerned, the Guinness Trust Holiday Home was the right building in the right place at the right time; history has proved that. If the enemy had discovered it, he would have plastered the locality, and me with it! During the war I lived at the bottom of the hill adjacent to the public right of way which led past the Guinness Trust building to Newhaven. My bedroom in those days commanded a very nice outlook of the unspoiled hillside with the Holiday Home on the top, not a quarter of a mile away.

The only evidence that the Guinness Trust Holiday Home was once used for military purposes is a commemorative plaque above the fireplace in the main hall. On this plaque, is a Crown flanked by two dates, 20 JUNE 1940 and 31 AUGUST 1945, with ROYAL NAVAL HEADQUARTERS inscribed beneath. One other date, covertly recorded by the bricklayer who built the wall which sealed the top entrance of the tunnel read 21 November, 1945, a certain indicator that the property was still in the hands of the Ministry of Works at this time and had not yet been returned to its rightful owners.

After its release by the Ministry, the building reverted to its former purpose until recreational habits changed. Following a period of disuse it was leased by the WRVS as a Residential Club for the Elderly and renamed DENTON HOUSE during the 1960s and remained so until about 1988 when

*Denton House Hall showing commemorative plaque above fireplace.*

(Geoffrey Ellis, 10 December 1992)

*Close up of commemorative plaque.*

(Geoffrey Ellis, 10 December 1992)

changes in governmental financing led to the abolition of this lease. Although reputedly a draughty place, it was very popular with the elderly tenants on account of its situation, and there were some very distressing scenes as these folk were removed from the premises.

Up until this time HMS FORWARD ship's bell had remained a feature in the lounge, but it was carefully packed and returned to the Admiralty by some of the old folk and has subsequently vanished! It seems it was a very collectible artifact. Fortunately, the Guinness Trust Head Office still retains HMS FORWARD ship's visitor's book which contains a number of wartime VIP signatures.

Denton House was vacant for many years after 1988 and subject to constant vandalism. It is to the discredit of our society that the building could not be used economically and remained empty. The most distressing news was that Denton House was under consideration for demolition. It was proposed to raze it to the ground to make way for more abominable character-less constructions which appeal more to the Estate accountants than the local populace!

The news of the pending demolition prompted Newhaven Historical Society to approach the Guinness Trust to seek permission to open up the former entrance to the tunnel through the floor of room 16. Happily they agreed to our request on condition that no publicity was accorded to our investigations until the tunnel had been resealed as a precaution against further vandalism.

In 1995, repeated planning applications were announced by Lewes District Council in the local press as follows, (with minor amendments), "South Heighton. Denton House. Demolition of existing bungalows and single-storey wings to Denton House for the erection of twenty-nine houses and the conversion of Denton House to provide six flats and community facilities with associated car parking and landscaping. Guinness Trust SE (Southern) Area."

Whilst in essence the more architecturally interesting parts of the building are to be preserved, the character of what remains will be destroyed together with its aspect ratio. And with it, will disappear a little more of our more pleasant heritage.

On Monday, 26 February, 1996, Messrs Wilmott Dixon arrived on site to commence demolition. It was then learned that Messrs Mackellar Schwerdt Partnership (Architects) had been most sympathetic to the existence of the tunnel, and had made provision to provide ventilation facilities which will be of considerable future benefit.

STATISTICS.
TOTAL LENGTH OF ACCESS GALLERIES    350 yds.
    "    "    " LARGE    "    200 yds.

TOTAL VOLUME OF ACCESS GALLERIES  1600 cu yds.
        $(= 1220 \text{ m}^3$ or  1,220,000 litres$)$.

TOTAL VOLUME OF LARGE GALLERIES  1650 cu yds.
        $(= 1264 \text{ m}^3$ or  1,264,000 litres$)$.

SOLID CHALK INCREASES ITS VOLUME BY HALF
WHEN DUG. SOME 5700 TONS OF SPOIL HAD
TO BE DISPOSED OF WHEN EXCAVATING THIS
LABYRINTH.

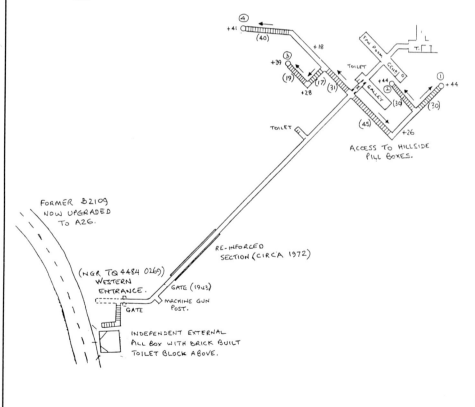

N

ACCESS TO HILLSIDE
PILL BOXES.

FORMER B2109
NOW UPGRADED
TO A26.

RE-INFORCED
SECTION (CIRCA 1972)

(NGR TQ 4484 0269)
WESTERN
ENTRANCE.    GATE (1943)

GATE    MACHINE GUN
    POST.

INDEPENDENT EXTERNAL
PILL BOX WITH BRICK BUILT
TOILET BLOCK ABOVE.

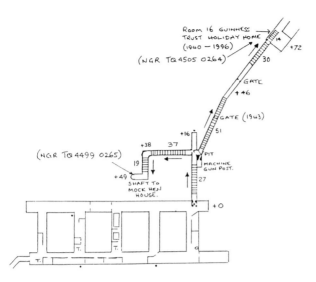

Room 16 GUINNESS
TRUST HOLIDAY HOME
(1940 — 1996)
+72
30
(NGR TQ4505 0264)

GATE
+ +6

GATE (1943)

+16
51
+38  37
(NGR TQ 4499 0265)
PIT
19
MACHINE
GUN POST.
+49
SHAFT TO
MOCK HEN
HOUSE.
27

+O

T.
T.
T.

NOTES.

1.  PLUS FIGURES (+16) INDICATE HEIGHT ABOVE
    OPERATIONS AREA FLOOR LEVEL, IN FEET.

2.  FIGURES AGAINST STAIRWAYS INDICATE
    NUMBER OF CONCRETE STAIRS. FIGURES
    IN PARENTHESIS INDICATE ESTIMATED
    NUMBER OF FORMER WOODEN STAIRS.

3.  CIRCLED FIGURES INDICATE HILL SIDE
    PILL BOXES.

    0   20   40   60   80   100

    Scale ~ Feet.

HEIGHTON HILL, NEWHAVEN
FORMER WW2 SUBTERRANEAN
NAVAL OPERATIONS INTELLIGENCE
CENTRE.   1941 — 1945.
ABANDONED  21 NOV 1945.

© G.ELLIS   4 JAN 1996.

*Plan of tunnel. Entire Labyrinth.*
(Geoffrey Ellis, 4 January 1996)

# TECHNICAL DATA

## National Grid References

The following data gives information relating to the subterranean installation acquired from measurements and references to Ordnance Survey Plans TQ 4402 & TQ 4502 Scale 1:2500, and Ordnance Survey Plans TQ4402NE & TQ4502NW Scale 1:1250.

Many of the features which originally reached the surface have already (in 1993) been hidden by subsequent development. This information indicates what existed at the following locations. No information is available to indicate the current depth of these features, nor how they have been covered.

Tunnel East End (Denton House) ........................ TQ 4505 0264 Concrete Steps

Tunnel West End (Beddingham Road) ................. TQ 4484 0269 Reinforced Portal

Mock Chicken House Pillbox ................................. TQ 4499 0265 Square Manhole

Hillside Pillbox No. 1 (South) ............................. TQ 4495 0265 Square Manhole

Hillside Pillbox No. 2 ........................................... TQ 4494 0266 Square Manhole

Hillside Pillbox No. 3 ........................................... TQ 4492 0269 Square Manhole

Hillside Pillbox No. 4 (North) ............................ TQ 4492 0271 Square Manhole

Antenna Feed Pipe No. 1 (SW) .......................... TQ 4497 0263 3·5ins iron pipe

Antenna Feed Pipe No. 2 (NW) .......................... TQ 4496 0265 3·5ins iron pipe

Antenna Feed Pipe No. 3 (NE) ........................... TQ 4497 0266 3·5ins iron pipe

Public Electricity Feed Pipe ................................ TQ 4502 0265 3·5ins iron pipe

Engine Exhaust Outlet .......................................... TQ 4494 0266 10·5ins dia duct

Ventilation Air Exhaust ........................................ TQ 4499 0262 12ins dia duct

Should any of these features be subsequently discovered, it is recommended that they are permanently 'capped' with masonry. Any attempt to infill will be unsatisfactory on account of the size of the voids beneath and settlement.

The floor level of the operations centre and the western entrance is estimated to be 72ft below the Denton House Bench Mark of 98·44ft (29·99m) AOD. The closest Bench Mark to the western end of the tunnel is at the bottom of the Hollow where a level of 15·39ft (4·67m) AOD is indicated.

# BIBLIOGRAPHY

*War Plan UK*
  Duncan Campbell, Paladin books, ISBN 0-586-08479-7

*GCHQ — The Secret Wireless War 1900–86*
  Nigel West, Coronet books, ISBN 0-340-41197-X

*Britannia's Daughters*
  Ursula Stuart Mason, Redwood Press, ISBN 0-85052-271-4

*WRNS History Book*
  Dame MH Fletcher, Batsford 1989, ISBN 0-713-46185-3


The following records at the Public Records Office, Ruskin Avenue, KEW, were researched to provide material for this article.

DEFE2/855
  Status of Newhaven as an Operational base 1941–42.

ADM1/13106
  Newhaven Naval Headquarters protective arrangements 1942-3.

ADM1/18136
  Newhaven Sub-command. (HMS FORWARD). History of war activities. 1945.

# ACKNOWLEDGEMENTS

I am indebted to Guinness Estate Manager Mr Peter Vandenbegin (Local Guinness Estates Manager), Chris Knight (Area Manager) and the Trustees of the Guinness Estate at Head Office for their kind permission and assistance in allowing the Newhaven Historical Society a period of unrestricted access to Denton House to research this project. Their cooperation enabled this investigation to proceed in a manner which few would have believed possible.

Mention must be made of the motivation and assistance given by Mr Peter Bailey, Hon Curator of Newhaven Historical Society. Peter's enthusiasm provided the catalyst which rekindled my long-standing ambition.

I am also grateful to Tom Bonnor of Brooks Video Communications for his time and services, given gratuitously, in compiling spectacular video material and providing numerous photographic stills. Thanks are recorded to those who loaned cables, flood lights and disco lamps with which the galleries were illuminated to an extent not witnessed in nearly fifty years (or ever?).

My thanks also go to Cyril Leister, Arthur Smith and Harry Mitchell for their assistance in surveying and recording, and the less than desirable task of removing all the decaying silt from the drained pit. The stench this produced is undescribable; however, the evidence revealed in the floor enabled an accurate layout of the former equipment to be drawn.

Tributes are due to my ex-professional colleagues, Len Miller and Dennis Tompsett, whose memories and anecdotes proved invaluable.

I am indebted to the considerable number of ex-service personnel, mainly WRNS, whose response to my appeals in many magazines, newspapers and national radio produced information and photographs which contributed immensely to the knowledge and understanding of this establishment, and its operation. Without their authentic first-hand information, this report would have been conjecture.

My initial ambition was purely to acknowledge for posterity the contribution of the tunnel, built and used specifically for the Defence of the Realm in World War II. However, as my research progressed it became abundantly clear that the tunnel was inextricably woven into the military defence infrastructure, and did not stand in isolation. In attempting to maintain faith with my objective I realise that I have excluded some duties performed by HMS FORWARD.

*Geoffrey Ellis*

# VETERANS ROLL OF HONOUR

The author wishes to acknowledge his gratitude to the following RN and WRNS veterans who volunteered information contributing towards a greater understanding of this establishment, enabling both this book and the complementary video to be produced for posterity.

Mrs Delphine Crowlie (nee Foster), Coder (1942);
Mrs Joyce "Mitch" Kitson (nee Mitchell), Coder (Late '44 to 07-45);
Mrs Tresina "Trixie" Gell (nee Williams), Plotter (09-42 to 07-45);
Miss Masie Hill, Plotter (08-44 for a few weeks);
Mrs Eleanor Thornhill (nee Hoey), Plotter (1941/42);
Mrs Yvonne Hastie Groves (nee Parker), Sigs Dist Office (09-06-41 to 14-10-43);
Mrs Nancy Thompson (nee Longstaff), Sigs Dist Office (02-44 to 07-45);
Mrs Peggy Bentley (nee Matthews), Sigs Dist Office (1944/45);
Mrs Joan Pillar (nee Gilder), Sigs Dist Office (09-11-44 to 17-08-45);
Mrs Eileen Dean (nee Smart), Sigs Dist Office (1944/45);
Mrs Violet Coles (nee Bedwell), SDO Telephonist (1944/45);
Miss Pauline Tipler, Switchboard Operator (01-44 to 07-45);
Mrs Peggy Gait (nee Coles), Switchboard Opr (1943/45);
Mrs Betty Storey (nee Connell), Teleprinter Opr (06-44 onwards);
Mrs Renee Peett (nee Beretta), Teleprinter Opr. (06-44 onwards);
Mrs Marguerite Curtis (nee Humphreys), Telegraphist. (03-44 to 07-45);
Mrs Betty Sievey (nee Smith), Telegraphists (1944);
Vic Sievey, Telegraphist (1944);
Cyril "Cigs" Taylor, Telegraphist (1944);
Reg Cannan, Telegraphist (1944).

Whilst not employed within the tunnel, the following ex-WRNS provided useful information.

Mrs Doris N Pearce (nee Turner), Captains Office (1944/45);
Mrs Amy Cowgill (nee Cooper), Driver (03-42 to 03-43);
Miss Marjorie Hervey, Driver (1942/43);
Mrs Kathleen Howe (nee Woodger), Officers Cook L&P Hotel (1941/43);
Mrs Doreen M Coles, Harbour area (Early to mid '44);
Miss Freda Flowers, Boats Crew (06-09-43 to 31-12-44);
Mrs Dora Williamson (nee Keep), Officers Quarters (1941/45)

I learned of the following WRNS from their shipmates listed above, however I have been unsuccessful in contacting them to date. Many others served here also, but their names are not currently known.

Audrey De Beaufort; Clarice Behar, Messenger; Lynn Bignell; Doreen Breech, Plotter; Joyce Bridges; Clare Brown; Vivienne Burbridge; Norma Cecil; Mavis Cook; Joan Crew; Jill Crocker; Pat Devlin; June Done; Phyllis Fisher; Esther Galbraith; Gloria Goldstein; Sylvia Greener; P/O Grimwade; Mary Hill; Dorothy Hunt; Petty Officer Lambert-Hann; Pam Lawson; Christina McLellan; Jeanne Marks P/O, Plotter; Peggy Martin; Joan Morgan, Telegraphist; "Mickey" Mundy; "Nicky" Joan Nicholson, Telegraphist; Eileen Petherick; Kathy Phelps; Freda Rennison, Telegraphist; Janet Ross; Joan Rowlands; Dorothy Smart; Dorothy "Dippy" Smith; Wendy Talbot; Joan Tarry; Kathleen White; Margaret Woods.

The following WRNS who served with HMS FORWARD have been reported deceased. Their service with HMS FORWARD is acknowledged posthumously.

*Pat Buckingham; Irene Davies (Mrs Lewis), Telegraphist; Ruth Hall, Teleprinter Operator; Norah Heard, Teleprinter Operator.*